"The famous theologian Bernard Lonergan declared that reflection on spiritual transformation is the new foundation for genuine religious living. Dennis Dempsey provides us with a unique, deep look into two worlds: Alcoholics Anonymous and the Catholic Church. His narrative reveals the profound action of grace on his own self-destructive addiction, and the role that religious experience played in pivoting him into a new life. His story reveals his own attempt to integrate the spirituality of his twelve-step program with his re-commitment and rediscovery of his childhood Catholic faith. This is an honest, captivating account from someone who has been to Hell and back."

—JOHN DADOSKY, Professor of Philosophy and Theology, Regis-St. Michaels, University of Toronto

"This book is an intriguing testimony of how faith is at the same time an intellectual as well as an existential journey. It is marvelously written and combines the skills of brilliant storytelling with substantial theological reflection. Moreover, especially today it tells us how the Christian belief in a living God who reveals his mercy in Christ is intimately connected to a love for the church."

—THOMAS SCHÄRTL-TRENDEL, Chair of Fundamental Theology, Ludwig Maximilian University of Munich

"I cried reading *Alcohol Was My God*. I felt the hopelessness of the author in his darkest moments but also the helplessness of the people who loved him. If there is one message to take from this honest and non-romanticized account from alcohol addiction to living 'one day at a time,' it is that hope, love, and faith are always waiting to embrace us, to re-embrace us, and to be embraced and re-embraced by us."

—CRISTINA LLEDO GOMEZ, Senior Lecturer, The Australian Institute of Theological Education

"In this honest, moving narrative, Dennis Dempsey weaves the strands of Alcoholics Anonymous, his own story, and his Catholic faith into a tapestry that shows how grace works in a particular life. Admirably holding the messy realities of all three in tension, *Alcohol Was My God* probes the theological resonances of AA, making clear to this reader that there is much the Catholic Church could and should learn from AA."

—M. THERESE LYSAUGHT, Professor, Neiswanger Institute for Bioethics and Health Policy, Stritch School of Medicine, Loyola University Chicago

Alcohol Was My God

Alcohol Was My God

A Catholic Alcoholic Reflects on His Faith

DENNIS DEMPSEY

RESOURCE *Publications* • Eugene, Oregon

ALCOHOL WAS MY GOD
A Catholic Alcoholic Reflects on His Faith

Copyright © 2025 Dennis Dempsey. All rights reserved. Except for brief quotations in critical publications or reviews, no part of this book may be reproduced in any manner without prior written permission from the publisher. Write: Permissions, Wipf and Stock Publishers, 199 W. 8th Ave., Suite 3, Eugene, OR 97401.

Resource Publications
An Imprint of Wipf and Stock Publishers
199 W. 8th Ave., Suite 3
Eugene, OR 97401

www.wipfandstock.com

PAPERBACK ISBN: 979-8-3852-3885-9
HARDCOVER ISBN: 979-8-3852-3886-6
EBOOK ISBN: 979-8-3852-3887-3

03/14/25

Scripture quotations are from The Catholic Edition of the Revised Standard Version of the Bible, copyright © 1965, 1966 National Council of the Churches of Christ in the United States of America. Used by permission. All rights reserved worldwide.

The Twelve Steps and the Twelve Traditions are reprinted with permission of Alcoholics Anonymous World Services, Inc. ("A.A.W.S."). Permission to reprint the Twelve Steps and the Twelve Traditions does not mean that A.A.W.S. has reviewed or approved the contents of this publication, or that A.A. necessarily agrees with the views expressed herein. A.A. is a program of recovery from alcoholism only - use of the Twelve Steps and Twelve Traditions in connection with programs and activities which are patterned after A.A., but which address other problems, or in any other non-A.A. context, does not imply otherwise. Additionally, while A.A. is a spiritual program, A.A. is not a religious program. Thus, A.A. is not affiliated or allied with any sect, denomination, or specific religious belief.

Contents

Acknowledgments   vii

Part One—Background

REFLECTION 1: The Spark and the Engine   3
REFLECTION 2: Why I Don't Use My Real Name   7
REFLECTION 3: Why I Write   11
REFLECTION 4: A.A. and the Catholic Church   15
REFLECTION 5: Spirituality and Religion   19

Part Two—Alcohol Was My God

REFLECTION 6: The Darkness—High School   25
REFLECTION 7: The Darkness—College   28
REFLECTION 8: Probing the Darkness   32
REFLECTION 9: My First A.A. Meeting   36
REFLECTION 10: Touched by God's Presence   39

Part Three—A Ninety Day Wonder Grows Rapidly Then Relapses

REFLECTION 11: Was It Really God Who Became Present to Me?   45
REFLECTION 12: Are There Just Two Kinds of People in the World?   49

CONTENTS

REFLECTION 13: Reading the Gospels	54
REFLECTION 14: Seeking the Will of God	57
REFLECTION 15: Diving Back into Drinking and Denial	62

Part Four—Making My Way Back Both to A.A. and the Catholic Church

REFLECTION 16: Confession Followed by an A.A. Meeting	69
REFLECTION 17: Why I Needed A.A.	72
REFLECTION 18: A Shaky Re-Entry into the Catholic Church's Atmosphere	76
REFLECTION 19: Balancing Factors	81
REFLECTION 20: Why I Needed the Catholic Church	85

Part Five—From Rigidity to Open-Minded Inquiry

REFLECTION 21: Defender of the Faith	91
REFLECTION 22: Forging My Catholic Identity through Encounters with Evangelicals	96
REFLECTION 23: At Home in a Challenging Catholic Learning Environment	101
REFLECTION 24: Discerning the Presence of the Holy Spirit	105
REFLECTION 25: Are You Talking to Me?	110

Part Six—Personal Synthesis

REFLECTION 26: The God of My Understanding Who Remains Beyond my Comprehension	115
REFLECTION 27: Spiritual Growth Is Central to Theology	121
REFLECTION 28: Three Meanings of "Synthesis"	127
REFLECTION 29: More on the Third Meaning of "Synthesis"	132
REFLECTION 30: Alcohol Is No Longer My God	135

CONTENTS

APPENDIX 1: The Twelve Steps of Alcoholics Anonymous   139
APPENDIX 2: The Twelve Traditions of Alcoholics
    Anonymous (short form)   141
Bibliography   143

Acknowledgments

I THANK FIRST OF all my wife, who read the manuscript many times with a keen editorial eye. I also thank my children who read it and commented. In addition, I thank others who gave me feedback and encouragement: Matt Clemons, John Dadosky, Ottmar Edenhofer, Christina Gschwandtner, Hans Hafner, David Hammond, Mark Higgins, and Thomas Schärtl-Trendl.

PART ONE

Background

REFLECTION 1

The Spark and the Engine

I WAS TWENTY-TWO WHEN I first joined Alcoholics Anonymous. After about one hundred days, I relapsed for two months. On August 25, 1975, I returned. I've been a continuously sober member of A.A. for nearly fifty years. The same day that I went back to A.A., I also returned to the Catholic Church, from which I had lapsed. My faith in God became the most important thing in my life. Eventually, I earned a doctorate in theology and worked as a professor at a Catholic university for four decades.

I got high on alcohol for the first time when I was fourteen. By the age of sixteen, I had a drinking problem. I earned a reputation among my peers in high school and throughout my college years as a drunk.

There is a Lutheran theologian, Paul Tillich (1886–1965), who taught that faith is a matter of ultimate concern. I learned from him the idea that, whatever it is that functions for you as the most important thing in your life, that is your God.[1] During the years of my drinking, alcohol was my God.

This book is about how A.A. and the Catholic Church worked in tandem in the early years of my sobriety to set me on a path of spiritual growth. It is about how I needed each of these communities. It is about how I benefited both from ways in which they

---

1. Tillich, *Dynamics of Faith*, 12.

overlapped as well as from ways in which they differed. The format is somewhat like a testimony I could give in an A.A. meeting.

One important difference is that in A.A., out of respect for its being "spiritual but not religious," I would not give explicit witness to my Catholic faith. Another important difference lies in the level of religious and theological analysis in which I engage. Still, this book is not a treatise in Catholic theology. It does not pretend to give an overview of Catholic teaching about God or any other theological topic. This book is my witness to the transformation that took place in my life, and to the mutually reverberating roles that A.A. and the Catholic Church played in that transformation.

This is a book that had been building up inside of me for many decades. It is a book that I had to write.

Theme One: The Initial Spark

A.A. provided the spiritual spark that allowed my Catholic engine to get restarted. I can hardly imagine returning to the Catholic Church without the spiritual awakening that I received as a gift from God through my working of the Twelve Step program.[2] When I examine my A.A. experience through the lens of my Catholic faith, I can say that it was through A.A. that I first acquired a felt awareness of the presence within me of the Holy Spirit, the divine spirit of truth and love.

Still today, if I think about where I encounter the Holy Spirit, A.A. meetings are the first thing that comes to mind. Such is my own personal discernment. Although in A.A. there is plenty of talk about God, there is no mention of the Holy Spirit or of Jesus Christ or of anything trinitarian.

I believe that even though one can truly experience the Holy Spirit within oneself, the Holy Spirit's main arena of operation is not simply within an individual but among people as a dynamic guiding presence on various levels and in various types of groups such as a meeting, a community, an authoritative body, or a global

---

[2]. See Appendix 1.

initiative. Recognizing the work of the Holy Spirit takes careful, humble discernment, for there are many things in life that claim to be good or true or holy or loving that are anything but.

Rather than refer to Holy Spirit, A.A. members speak of a "group conscience" that guides each meeting. If a decision needs to be made, the meeting leader will consult the group conscience, which is the collective wisdom of those present. The group conscience is also thought to inform the overall tenor of a meeting, such that even if one or two members say things that are out of tune with the A.A. program, the overall meaning that emerges from all the voices together will virtually always be a message that can be trusted.

A.A. set me off on a spiritual journey. The Twelve Steps inspired me to believe in God as a power greater than myself. I gave myself over to God, confessed my sins, and asked to have my character defects removed. I tried to make up for my transgressions. I learned to continue to examine my conscience, pray, and reach out to others. Were it not for A.A., I doubt that I would be alive today.

Theme Two: The Engine that Got Restarted

A.A. got me reinterested in God. As I explored the Bible and then read Catholic literature, I had many personal insights into the meaning of things that I had previously taken for granted. It was a matter of moving from a merely intellectual understanding to a deeply felt, even passionate, personal understanding. A young person who has not yet fallen in love might have some understanding of what it means to say, "I love you." If, however, that person were to fall deeply in love, then saying the phrase "I love you" can take on a whole new depth of meaning.

I sometimes learn what I am thinking when I hear myself saying it out loud to another person. I once observed myself spontaneously explaining to another person that my rediscovery of my faith was like the final scene of the film, *National Treasure*. At the end of a long quest, the seekers finally come upon a hidden room that lights up from a fire that travels along trenches of oil to reveal countless, priceless treasures. Then suddenly the fire spreads to light up another room filled with additional countless, priceless treasures. And then another. And then another. And on and on.

I have discovered in Catholic faith, tradition, and community riches beyond my wildest imagination. The Catholic faith opens up to me the basic story of what life is about. Catholic tradition offers me resources of inspiration and wisdom. Catholic community gives me formation, support, and a network of companions that stretches spatially across the globe, temporally across eternity, and transcendentally between the heavens and the earth. It has provided me with a worldview that enabled me to make my family my vocation and to make my life's work my ministry.

One can also find in Catholic history as well as present experience not only rooms that light up, but also rooms permeated by darkness. One can encounter darkness in A.A. too. After decades of sobriety and faith-filled living, I am additionally aware of dark chambers that remain within myself. In *Alcoholics Anonymous*, what we call the "Big Book," there is a saying: "we claim spiritual progress rather than spiritual perfection."[3]

In the reflections that follow, I focus on interconnections and contrasts between A.A. and the Catholic Church as these great organizations have impacted my life, especially in my first eight years of sobriety.

---

3. *Alcoholics Anonymous*, 60.

REFLECTION 2

Why I Don't Use My Real Name

WHATEVER IS SET DOWN in words is written in a particular time and place by a particular person. There may be such a thing as timeless truth, but even timeless truth is expressed in a time-bound way. It can be important, especially in a work that is quite personal, to know something about the author and where he or she is coming from.

I told you a few things about myself in the first reflection. I won't tell you my real name because I make explicit references to my membership in Alcoholics Anonymous. I see no way of not mentioning my membership. I am quite reconciled to the path of abiding by the traditions of Alcoholics Anonymous regarding anonymity.

In addition to the Twelve Steps, A.A. has Twelve Traditions.[1] Each tradition has a short form and a long form. The short form of Tradition Eleven reads: "Our public relations policy is based on attraction rather than promotion; we need always maintain personal anonymity at the level of press, radio, and films."[2] Since I am writing for public consumption, I am expected to maintain my personal anonymity.

---

1. See Appendix 2.
2. *Alcoholics Anonymous*, 562.

Alcohol Was My God—Part One

I have had some minor difficulty explaining to colleagues why I am writing a work without using my full name. After all, in the academic world, publications are closely linked with promotions and merit pay. Isn't there some way around that requirement? In many cases, authors write about being a recovering alcoholic without explicitly mentioning that they are A.A. members. In this case, however, my precise topic is the interaction between A.A. and the Catholic Church as they have impacted my life.

Otherwise, I frequently and happily tell people that I am a member of A.A. Anyone who knows me personally knows this about me. Just about every student who has ever had me for a class knows this. On many occasions, people have sought out my advice or help regarding alcoholism either for themselves or for someone close to them. Not revealing that I am a recovering alcoholic would be like hiding my light under a bushel basket (see Matt 5:14). A.A. has a Responsibility Statement that I used to carry around with me on a small card: "I am responsible, when anyone, anywhere, reaches out for help, I want the hand of A.A. always to be there, and for that I am responsible."

I find no contradiction in the directives to make myself available, but on certain levels to maintain personal anonymity. The principle of anonymity serves several purposes, of which I will focus on two. The first is that someone who is considering joining A.A. needs to know that their identity will be kept secret. Active alcoholics carry with them a load of shame and rightfully fear the social stigma attached to alcoholism. Many would not even consider joining if they thought it would become public knowledge. Potential members must feel confident that the term "Anonymous," found in the very title of our organization, will apply strictly and seriously to them.

There is noticeably less social stigma attached to alcoholism in the United States than when I joined in 1975. Yet social stigma remains, especially for those still actively drinking or those who have only recently begun their recovery. As someone with five decades in the program, I often get the reaction from people that they think that by joining A.A. I have done something admirable and courageous. I always say that it was my pain that drove me to seek out help and that my recovery is a gift from God. A.A. has taught me that when I see a person who is still suffering from their alcoholism, I should think: there but for the grace of God go I. Over the years, the topic of recovery has been amply treated in television, films, and literature. Most people are willing to accept the A.A. model of treating alcoholism as a disease. People in recovery are even sometimes presented as cultural heroes.

The second major purpose of the principle of anonymity on which I will focus is a spiritual one designed to combat the self-seeking of personal honor and recognition. The short form of Tradition Twelve reads: "Anonymity is the spiritual foundation of all our traditions, ever reminding us to place principles above personalities."[3] Members are not to use their A.A. experience as a launching pad to fame and glory. The longer form of Tradition Twelve adds: "that we are actually to practice a genuine humility. This is to the end that our great blessings may never spoil us; that we shall forever live in thankful contemplation of Him who presides over us all."[4]

My A.A. experience has led me to pay special attention to the principle of anonymity as expressed by Jesus in the Sermon on the Mount, when he says, "Beware of practicing your piety before others in order to be seen by them; for then you have no reward from your Father in heaven" (Matt 6:1). In the passages that follow, Jesus makes several similar points. St. Paul echoes several places in the Old Testament when he writes, "Let the one who boasts, boast in the Lord" (2 Cor 10:17).

In my studies of mid-twentieth century Catholic theologians whose works led up to the Second Vatican Council (1962–65), I noticed how occasionally they put forth ideas that originated with other Catholic theologians without citing sources. My sense was that they were doing the opposite of stealing ideas for their own advancement. These theologians were operating self-consciously as part of an intellectual community that easily shared information

---

3. *Alcoholics Anonymous*, 562.
4. *Alcoholics Anonymous*, 566.

and that did not care much about keeping track of exactly who said what first. Most of these theologians belonged to religious orders such as the Jesuits and the Dominicans. They stressed personal humility over self-promotion.

The teaching of the Second Vatican Council stressed the need for humility in the Church, its leaders, and all followers of Christ. These teachings square well with the spirit of A.A.. Humility, however, does not always call for anonymity; sometimes it requires taking your light out from under a bushel basket.

REFLECTION 3

Why I Write

I MENTIONED EARLIER HOW I sometimes find out what I am thinking when I hear what I am saying to someone else. In 1984, I had an interview with a religious studies department faculty for the position which I have held for four decades. The first part of the interview was structured around my formally addressing academic theological questions that had been mailed to me beforehand. The second part was less structured, with faculty members asking me a range of questions designed to pull me out and probe me as a person. I vaguely remember that I gave good answers and was also pretty funny. Everyone was in a good mood. At one point, I mentioned being a recovering alcoholic with eight years of sobriety. Then one professor asked me if I could state a goal or vision that would express what I am really all about. My spontaneous reply was something that I had never before said aloud or even thought: "I'd like to make the Catholic Church be more like A.A."

The room erupted in laughter. From a couple of comments that were made, I could see that they connected what I was saying with something that was generally true at that time about Catholic universities and Catholic events in general when compared to Protestant and even secular settings. Catholics always seemed to have plenty of liquor around. It is only a slight exaggeration to say that many faculty meetings and various other occasions were not all that different from happy hour at a local bar. Over the past few decades, that situation has changed gradually but dramatically.

In the course of U.S. history, though, Catholic immigrants were the lower class and often thought of as drunkards by the upper crust. Prohibition was in many ways directed at Catholics. Catholics, if I may over-generalize, tended to be proud of their non-teetotaler status as well as of their ability to hold their liquor. Providing sufficient amounts of beer and whiskey was an important part of the preparation for large family gatherings, whether for wakes, weddings, christenings, first communions, confirmations, anniversaries, or birthday parties. The very thought of making the Catholic Church more like A.A. struck the 1984 religious studies faculty of a Catholic university as hilarious.

I'm pretty sure that none of them thought that I meant my remark in the way that they took it. The humor had as much to do with the situation and the timing as with the meaning of the words I spoke. It's like here's this guy who already established his credentials and shared something of his personality. He already delivered a couple of laugh lines. Now he tells us that he's a recovering alcoholic. And then he says that he wants to make the Catholic Church be more like A.A. What a riot!

Yet I had intended my response to be serious. I wasn't at all disappointed that they laughed. Although when they hired me it was not because I am funny, the humor didn't hurt.

This idea of making the Catholic Church be more like A.A. will help me to talk about why I am writing these reflections. My goals are not so narrowly defined. I think it would be arrogant of me to have as a main objective a set design about how I would want to remake the Catholic Church according to A.A. Yet, if I may say so humbly, there is an element of that in the mix of my intentions.

It's more to my overall purpose in writing these reflections to say that when I was a young man something really big happened to me to change my life. That really big thing had to do with recovery from alcoholism through A.A. and through my reembrace of my Catholic faith. For me, these two things happened together in a way that is deeply intertwined. I need to ponder these things for myself and share my insights with others. Alcoholics Anonymous and the Catholic Church have echoed within the depths of my being in a complementary fashion throughout the course of my life. Personally, I needed both. Each of them continually gives me some perspective on the other.

So, what did I mean when I blurted out my vision at my job interview? I was thinking about how A.A. had been able to bring me experientially from a state of darkness into light. It offered me a community of support and a program that opened up the opportunity for me to stop drinking (one day at a time) and to start growing through faith, self-examination, repentance, prayer, and helping others. I had been in a very bad way, deeply sick. From the moment I joined, A.A. gave me hope by naming my disease and proclaiming that there is a way out of the madness.

I knew from my Catholic upbringing that there was plenty of talk in the Christian faith about the kinds of things that I actually experienced in A.A. I wanted the Catholic Church to channel its sacred power through small Christian communities or faith groups that could take in people with all kinds of sins and all manner of problems and help them to turn their lives around and find God. That is what I was thinking at the time of my job interview. Today I want to add that the Catholic Church has many characteristics that are different from A.A. that I don't want to change. I will be addressing this topic further in later reflections.

In 2002, though, many years after that job interview, I found myself in a situation that reminded me, at least in some respects, that I did wish that the Catholic Church might be more like A.A. I travelled to Hawaii to teach a graduate course over a three-week period. Early on in my stay, I went to an A.A. event and met several people. Then I attended a couple of meetings. After that I gave a lead (told my story) at a large meeting held on Waikiki Beach. It quickly got to be that I could hardly walk down a street without one or two people calling out my name and saying Aloha. By the time I left, I had made many personal connections.

It struck me that, at least in my own experience, it would be unlikely to find such spontaneous community outreach and immediate support in the Catholic Church. I somehow wanted the Catholic Church to be more intimate, welcoming, immediate, inclusive, and transformative, but without losing its traditions, depth, quality, standards, and institutional power.

REFLECTION 4

A.A. and the Catholic Church

I NEED TO MAKE something clear before I go on so that there won't be any confusion. A.A. and the Catholic Church are two completely different things.

A.A. was founded in 1935 by Bill Wilson (1895–1971) and Dr. Bob (Robert Smith, 1879–1950). Its nature and purpose are described in the A.A. Preamble as "a fellowship of people who share their experience, strength and hope with each other that they may solve their common problem and help others to recover from alcoholism."[1] Today it is a global organization with more than 123,000 groups in 180 countries.

As institutions, A.A. and the Catholic Church have little to nothing to do with each other. Along with non-religious people, there were some Catholics and other Christians, especially a fellowship known as the Oxford Group, that influenced the formulation of the A.A. program in its formative years.[2] There is, however, no institutional affiliation in either direction. Some Catholics may at times advise someone with a drinking problem to join A.A., and many A.A. meetings take place in church buildings. A.A. groups rent spaces, pay for their own coffee, and do not accept outside contributions. As the A.A. Preamble states: "A.A. is not allied with

---

1. "The AA Preamble," 1.
2. "The Start and Growth of A.A.," 1.

any sect, denomination, politics, organization or institution; does not wish to engage in any controversy, neither endorses nor opposes any causes."[3]

In A.A.'s Big Book, the entire fourth chapter is devoted to agnostics and atheists.[4] Today the more acceptable term would be "non-religious persons." That chapter was not written as a concession to include a few non-believers. The book's authors estimated that in the earliest years about half of the membership fit into this category. They admitted that some of them had negative attitudes toward religion that may be connected with their alcoholic madness. They acknowledged that in many cases their respect for religion grew with their overall maturity. They even said to the chapter's audience of atheists and agnostics:

> We . . . beg you to put aside all prejudices, even against organized religion. We have learned that whatever the human frailties of various faiths may be, those faiths have given purpose and direction to millions. People of faith have a logical idea of what life is all about.

The authors do not, however, encourage members to join or not to join either a particular religion or any religion at all.

Rather than endorsing or opposing religion, the authors explain that it is possible for atheists and agnostics to have a spiritual experience and to learn to live their lives on a spiritual basis. They recognize the difficulty that talk of spirituality and of God can pose because many of them had to grapple with the same problem. They stress that the key for them was becoming willing to believe in a power greater than oneself. They acknowledge that no one can "fully define or comprehend that Power, which is God."[5] The recovering alcoholic, therefore, is not required to believe in God, even though the steps and much A.A. literature explicitly identify this higher power as God. It is God, that is, as that person understands God.

---

3. "The AA Preamble," 1
4. *Alcoholics Anonymous*, 44–57.
5. *Alcoholics Anonymous*, 46.

A.A. AND THE CATHOLIC CHURCH

I have often heard in meetings that, although the Twelve Steps do explicitly use the word, "God," it is only necessary, especially in the beginning, to believe in a power greater than oneself. Some alcoholics start out by taking the guidance of an A.A. group to be their higher power. An essential key to sobriety, after admitting that one has a problem in Step One, is Step Two: coming to believe that a power greater than ourselves can restore us to sanity.

I know some ex-Catholic recovering alcoholics who, to put it mildly, don't like the Catholic Church. On occasion, I have heard members in meetings make negative comments about the Catholic Church or about religion in general. I accept this. I have at times had my own negative experiences with both the Catholic Church and with religion. My response to such talk is to remind the group that we are here to share our experience, strength, and hope. If someone's negative comments about a church or about religion in general are coming out of their experience, they are right to share what they truly think and feel. I will also say, though, that such is their own experience and that it is not an official part of the A.A. program to make criticisms about religion. I will add that for me and for many other members, religion has played an important and positive role in our recovery. That too is not an official part of the A.A. program.

When I hear a member give an explicitly religious testimony in an A.A. meeting, I don't like it. I'm fine with people quoting the Bible or making a brief reference that obviously comes out of Christianity or some other religion, but I feel uneasy when someone declares that their sobriety comes from Jesus Christ their Redeemer or holds up a picture of a host and a chalice. I feel like they are violating the A.A. tradition of being spiritual but not religious. I do try to understand sympathetically where such a person is coming from. Such ideas and commitments are not far from my own heart. In an A.A. meeting, though, pointedly explicit witness is inappropriate because it is important not to proselytize or to force any particular religion on people.

In meetings, I often speak out of my faith, but without mentioning my religion. An exception is the rare occasion when I give a lead (tell my story at some length). Even then, I try to be careful not in any way to proselytize. I'm just sharing my own story while trying to be very clear that other people take other paths.

There are several different types of A.A. meetings. The most common type is the discussion meeting. Other meetings focus specifically on either the Big Book, the Twelve Steps, or the Twelve Traditions. Some meetings are listed as "Chairperson's Choice." There are also several types of what are called "lead" meetings. Often a member leads a meeting by telling their own story, which is then followed by comments and discussion.

One time, when I gave a lead in a town that was not my own, I was confronted and chastised by a member who said that A.A. liberated him from institutional religion and that he didn't come there to listen to such nonsense. Several other members spoke in my defense, explaining to my critic that I wasn't trying to push religion on anyone but just telling my own story. Later that night, I ran into a couple of people who had been at that meeting, and they apologized to me profusely.

I haven't conducted a survey, and so it is just my anecdotal opinion based on my personal observation that the number of A.A. members who do not belong to an established religion has been growing in recent years. This would not be surprising since the number of non-religious people in actual sociological surveys has been growing. Although it contradicts traditional A.A. terminology, I have heard lately a couple of members say that A.A. is their religion.

What I want to clarify in this reflection is that A.A. and the Catholic Church as institutions basically don't have anything to do with each other. Any and all connections that I will make between them have to do with my own personal lived experience. From my point of view, though, A.A. and the Catholic Church do share at least one important attribute: they are both gifts given by God to the human race. Although they have many elements of human invention, there is something momentous about each of them that goes beyond anything that human beings could simply have manufactured on their own.

REFLECTION 5

Spirituality and Religion

A.A. OPERATES WITH A strong distinction between "spirituality" and "religion." It was A.A.'s founder, Bill Wilson, who came up with the idea that the program would be "spiritual but not religious." This distinction works well, even brilliantly, within the A.A. context. Outside of the A.A. context, the distinction can be problematic. Both terms, "spirituality" and "religion," have a wide range of meanings. Yet the basic idea of being spiritual but not religious is widely embraced in many circles throughout the world today. In this reflection, I will explore some of the usefulness, complexities, and difficulties of this distinction.

In A.A., developing a relationship with one's higher power is called for in Step Three. The meaning of "spirituality" is connected with living one's life on the basis of a relationship with one's higher power. It is a matter of living according to the Twelve Steps. It is Step Three that gives the most direct and concise definition of the A.A. meaning of spirituality: "[We] made a decision to turn our will and our lives over to the care of God *as we understood Him*."[1]

Each of the Twelve Steps is important, but I have heard the most moving testimony again and again when members talk about taking Step Three. Step Three doesn't work without the previous two, but it is in itself a life-changer. It serves as a cornerstone of

---

1. *Alcoholics Anonymous*, 59.

what it means to live one's life on a spiritual basis. Taking Step Three gives the alcoholic a firm foothold from which to begin the ascent up the mountain of sobriety. It goes beyond mere belief in a higher power to forge a relationship with that higher power.

Step Three is something quite distinct and separate from one's decision to belong or not belong to an organized religion. "Spirituality" is thus sharply distinguished from established religious traditions such as Judaism, Christianity, Islam, and Buddhism. The intention behind such a sharp distinction is to make A.A. accessible to everyone no matter what religion they belong to or do not belong to. As contemporary society has become more and more pluralistic, this distinction now appeals to a wide range of people who have no connection with A.A. or any other Twelve Step program. "I'm spiritual but not religious" has become a calling card for many people who have left religion behind and yet still live in the pursuit of truth, goodness, justice, and ultimate meaning. It functions as a slogan defending the idea that just because a person does not belong to a traditional religion does not mean that they are not a good person.

The phrase "spiritual but not religious" fits well with the modern quest for authenticity. For many people in the world of today, what matters is not so much what you happen to be but rather that you be authentically whatever it is that you are. You can be a Jew, a Christian, a Muslim, a Buddhist, a nonreligious person, or whatever. Just don't be a hypocrite. Be who you are. Be authentic.

Where a problem arises for people who are traditionally religious, however, is that religion comes off here as at least implicitly something secondary to and less important than spirituality. This is true even in A.A.'s Big Book, which strives to explain the distinction in a way that is friendly to religion, arguing explicitly that religion should be recognized as a good thing whether or not one personally buys into it. In everyday speech, however, both within A.A. and in the larger world, the distinction is often used in a way that treats religion as either neutral or negative. Some people speak of spirituality with a look of reverence on their face, and then practically hold their nose and put their hand on their belly when they talk about religion.

Many traditionally religious people are wary of the phrase "spiritual but not religious" because they think it makes religion sound irrelevant. Even worse is that it can imply that religion has nothing to do with spirituality. Historically, however, both the words "spirituality" and "religion" as well as the realities to which they refer have been deeply and even essentially intertwined. When I was growing up, to say that a person is religious and to say that they are spiritual meant pretty much the same thing.

Language evolves. Words and their definitions vary widely over time and in different places. Biblical authors did not write about spirituality without religion, but they were very concerned about religion that lacked spirituality. They used numerous terms and images to distinguish between authentic religion and hypocritical religion. In the Book of Ezekiel, the moribund faith of the Israelites is described as dead bones that need to be brought back to life by the breath of God. In the Book of Amos, God bemoans the worthless rituals performed by a people who are not living a just life. In the Sermon on the Mount, Jesus criticizes hypocrites who perform rituals and do good works for the wrong reasons and praises those who live simply and humbly. The distinction is between the abuse of religion and religion lived rightly. In our contemporary terms, religion lived rightly is religion infused with spirituality.

The medieval theologian Thomas Aquinas (1225–1274), an Italian Dominican priest and scholar, distinguished between two ways of understanding the sacraments: as ritual acts and as the active channels of God's grace.[2] He associated religion with the performance of the ritual acts; he associated the life of grace, or spirituality, with sharing in the very life of God through faith, hope, and charity. For Aquinas, this distinction abstracted from things that were bound together in real life. Religion and the life of the spirit functioned as two sides of the same coin.

With the dawn of the modern world, such a distinction became sharpened into a separation in favor of what today we call

2. Aquinas, *Summa Theologiae*, III, 66, 1.

"spirituality" to the detriment of "religion." In the last year of the eighteenth century, the German Protestant theologian Friedrich Schleiermacher (1768-1834), known as the founding figure of modern, liberal theology, distinguished between, on the one hand, religious experience, defined as a consciousness of God manifested in a feeling of absolute dependence and, on the other hand, the things of religion such as doctrines, rituals, and codes of ethics.[3] In Schleiermacher's early work the things of religion are treated rather dismissively, though he corrected this tendency somewhat in his later writings. Many thinkers of the 19th and 20th centuries would build upon Schleiermacher's early work to distinguish sharply between some core spiritual element of Christianity and the less important things of religion.

The Russian novelist and scholar Leo Tolstoy (1828-1910), for example, contrasted the love, humility, and self-sacrifice exemplified by Jesus with the mere doctrines, rituals, and rules emphasized by the leaders of organized churches.[4] Tolstoy's approach underlies the framework upon which the contemporary distinction between "spirituality" and "religion" has been built.

The distinction works quite well in the A.A. context. Also, outside of A.A., the distinction opens up possibilities for many people to seek meaning in life apart from traditional organized religions. In important ways, it is possible today to be—I still need to put the words in quotation marks—"spiritual" without being "religious." Nonreligious people represent a large and growing group that needs to be respected. I remain wary, however, of the distinction being used to imply that religion is necessarily irrelevant or negative, or that religion itself has nothing to do with spirituality. Along with Thomas Aquinas, I find that in my own life spirituality and religion are two sides of the same coin.

---

3. Schleiermacher, *Speeches*, 26-101.
4. Tolstoy, *What I Believe,"* 4-13.

PART TWO

Alcohol Was My God

REFLECTION 6

The Darkness—High School

I REALLY WANT TO tell you about how I was carried out from the darkness into the light. In order to do that, I'll need to say some things about the darkness. I'll try to give you the basic picture, but I'm also going to be holding back a bit. Some of my children or grandchildren may read what I'm writing here. I am able to give details because I still possess a long Fourth Step (moral inventory) that I wrote out in the first several weeks of my sobriety.

I started drinking in high school, and from the first moment it was as though I had discovered a great friend. I felt so good. When I drank, I found that I could all of a sudden dance, talk to girls, and be funny in ways that I couldn't without my liquid companion. I was too shaky to shoot pool without having a few drinks, but after the third or fourth beer, I would get in the groove and put a few balls in the pockets.

The problem was that I rarely if ever would stop at a few beers. From my high school days until I joined A.A. about nine months after college, I was an active alcoholic.

My friends and I sometimes stole alcohol from our parents, but usually we bought it either from older kids who used a fake I.D. or from people over twenty-one. I would get away with drinking in high school because I would get drunk before a party, a dance, a movie, or a game, and would arrive home four or five hours after getting drunk. Often, when I came home, my parents would already be asleep.

When I was a high school junior, I was at a friend's house and drank a fifth of whiskey in twenty minutes. I passed out and threw up all over the back of his cellar. My friends took me home. One of them teased me about how my parents were going to get me. He used their first names. This infuriated me, and so I punched him. I did get caught by my parents that night and was grounded for a month. I later boasted to my peers about how much I had drunk.

A couple of months later, I stayed overnight at the same friend's house. His parents were out of town. I drank a fifth of cherry vodka in about an hour and a half. I passed out. After that, I know only what my friend told me. He put me in a chair and placed a T.V. dinner in front of me. I threw up all over it. Then he dragged me upstairs put me in a bathtub, and turned on the water completely cold, then scalding hot. I never moved. I woke up the next morning naked in a strange bed, not knowing where I was. I did not get caught by my parents that time. Again, I later bragged to my friends about how much I had drunk.

In my senior year of high school, my school lost a football game to a rival school on Thanksgiving. It was an away game. After the game, a large group of boys from the rival school were marching by and chanting, "We're number one!" I hollered out drunkenly, "Number one blowers!" I got the tar beat out of me. Luckily one of the group stepped in and stopped the beating before they killed me. My face was entirely swollen for several days. Again, I proudly recounted my adventure to whoever would listen.

Once I stopped by where I worked on my night off. I accidentally knocked over a cashier's till and spilled the money all over the floor. For some reason, I wanted to fight my boss. I told a co-worker friend to meet me later at a restaurant. He found me unconscious outside on the sidewalk. He then dragged me into a field and went to get help from our group of friends. Meanwhile, some friends of my older brother were in a garage close to that field. They found me running around the field screaming. I bragged to them about my sex life, even though it was non-existent. My own friends showed up at the field and started calling out my name, and my brother's friends handed me over to them. My parents had no difficulty recognizing my drunken condition that night. They grounded me again for a month.

Marijuana was popular in those days. I rarely smoked it and would tell people that I greatly preferred alcohol. One day, though, I smoked pot in the morning before my German class. My teacher, a priest, called on me to do the first fill-in-the-blank sentence of an exercise in the textbook. There was a fifty percent change of getting it right: should it be *hin* or *her* (as in *hingehen* or *herkommen*)? I got it wrong. He then had me do the next one. And then the next one. I was extraordinarily giddy and giggly. Altogether I got only one out of ten correct. The teacher detained me after class. He said that I had the ability to be one of the intellectual leaders of the community, but instead I was a childish screw-up.

I did date a few women in high school. My relationships never lasted more than three dates. The issue was always my drinking. In my senior year, I asked a girl who broke up with me what I could do. She said, "Stop drinking, Dennis. Stop drinking."

When later I was in a rehabilitation center and wrote out my moral inventory, I recognized that I engaged in a great deal of exhibitionism. I did things to shock people, enrage people, and draw attention to myself. I tended to be loud, vulgar, and obnoxious. I insulted or harassed women. I made jokes or comments of a sexual nature. Several times I got into fights with boys whose girlfriends I insulted. I often could not remember what I did afterward. I would hear later about what I did from others. My own friends were often angry with me, but their anger didn't stop me from drinking.

There are many other incidents from high school that I have left out. Some of those incidents are even more cringe-worthy than the ones I have told you about. Still, it felt to me that alcohol was my best friend, and I could not admit to myself that it was doing nothing but dragging me down into a realm of darkness,

REFLECTION 7

The Darkness—College

IN MY FIRST SEMESTER of college, I was still somewhat of a practicing Catholic, even though I had been growing away from my faith for some years. I was doing well in Math class, and I remember that a fellow student asked me to help him cheat. I agreed to do so for a case of beer. During the final exam, I wrote out the answers on a sheet of paper. As I got up to leave the room, I dropped the sheet on his foot. I suddenly felt a jolt in my conscience. In my Catholic mind, I thought I committed a mortal sin. I'm not sure, but I do think that act of dishonesty for a cache of alcohol may have been a turning point in my life. Until then, in spite of my alcoholic behavior, I was still trying to stay in a state of grace. After that cheating incident, I stopped going to Sunday Mass.

As a habitual drunk, I gradually came to cultivate a very casual relationship with truth. I can remember telling tall tales to people, especially girls my age, at parties or in bars. I once talked at length with a girl about my years in Vietnam, even though I had never been in the service. In the end, I told her I had been bullshitting her. She was not happy, but I thought our conversation had been funny and entertaining.

In my sophomore year of college, I went to see a counselor. I said that I thought that maybe I was an alcoholic. He asked me why I thought that. I replied that I was drunk most of the time and that I was spending about twenty or thirty dollars a week on alcohol.

He wanted to know if I might be interested in going to A.A., to which I answered, "I'm not *that* kind of an alcoholic." "Well," he asked, "what kind of an alcoholic are you?" I explained that I had underlying problems and talked about my general nervousness. He referred me to a psychiatric clinic at a different but nearby university. After a couple of sessions, that psychiatrist wanted me to join a therapy group, which, if I remember correctly, I refused because anyone who would be in such a group must be a very screwed up person. How could learning to talk in front of a group of screwed up people help one to relate to normal people? Of course, I could give a speech in front of screwed up people because who would care? After all, they were screwed up.

These thoughts that I have just shared were not normal. I was becoming a sick person, more and more withdrawn, and more and more of an egomaniac.

In college, as in high school, I did many, many embarrassing and self-humiliating things. I was spinning increasingly out of control and into the darkness. I drank before classes a few times, but I did most of my drinking in binges on weekends. I didn't belong to a fraternity, but I went to a lot of all-you-can-drink frat parties. Once I started to drink, I either would not or could not stop until I was smashed. On multiple occasions, I had a hangover that would last two or three days.

My life revolved around planning my drinking. In the opening reflection, I referred to a Lutheran theologian, Paul Tillich, who held that faith is a matter of ultimate concern. He wrote: "In true faith the ultimate concern is about the truly ultimate; while in idolatrous faith preliminary, finite realities are elevated to the rank of ultimacy."[1] I derived from this teaching the idea that, whatever it is that functions for you as the most important thing in your life, that is your God. These were the years during which alcohol was my God.

One summer day after I graduated college, I made a trip to New York City. I got drunk in my own city before I took a bus to the Port Authority terminal. Once I arrived, I went to the nearest

---

1. Tillich, *Dynamics of Faith*, 12.

bar and drank until it closed at 3:00 a.m. I had nowhere to go, and so I hailed a taxi and asked the driver to drop me off by a bench in Central Park. That morning, I woke up when an old man was feeling around my pockets. Then a young guy came and chased him away. My rescuer took me to where people whom I thought of as "stew bums" were sitting around. I hung out with them for several hours. I even bought some whiskey and shared it.

Then the guy who rescued me told me that he wanted me to have sex with his sister. I thought that meant that he was going to get a prostitute for me. He took me to a dilapidated building. The door to the building was not attached but rather leaned up against the doorframe. He led me upstairs to a room where there was nothing but a mattress. The "sister" never arrived. I fell asleep there for several hours. When I woke up, it was dark. I still had my return bus ticket and a little money. I made my way to the bus station and went home.

Probably the worst thing I did objectively speaking during my days of drinking was to drive a car blind drunk many dozens of times. I easily could have killed somebody. There were times when I would take a bus to a bar precisely so that I wouldn't drink and drive. After the bar closed at 2:00 a.m., I would take the bus home with a couple of six packs under my arm and then go driving around.

In the early 1970's, it was a lot easier to get away with drunk driving than it is now. Once I was driving down a major city avenue in the middle of the night using red lights as if they were stop signs. I was pulled over by the police. I was obviously drunk, and I apologized very politely to the officer who stood at my window. He had a fatherly concern for me. Instead of arresting me, he pointed to a diner about a block and a half up the street. He told me to go there and drink coffee until I was sober. I don't remember whether I actually got that cup of coffee or not.

A few hours later, at about five in the morning, I was stopped by the police in a neighborhood closer to the center city area because I was driving the wrong way on a one-way street. Again, I was super polite to the officer. I told him that I was going to the house of a college friend who lived a few blocks away. The officer made me promise that I would leave the car where they pulled me over and go to my friend's house to sleep it off. I did go to my friend's house, woke him up, and talked with him for about half an hour before I went back to my car and drove home. Those were different times than today when drunk driving is taken much more seriously.

After college I wanted to go to graduate school, but I decided to take a year off to earn some money. I was working a full-time job in a supermarket from 11:00 p.m. to 7:00 a.m. I drank every morning after work.

I was losing my friends. I experienced a devastating rejection from one of my closest pals from high school. I had thought I was going to be the best man at his wedding, but he called to tell me he wasn't even inviting me at all. I asked him what the problem was. He said, "You know what the problem is." I asked him again why he was disinviting me. He said, "It has to do with your character" and hung up.

My girlfriend and I got an apartment together, but, after a few months, she threw me out because of my drinking. I moved back in with my parents. Around that time, I was flagged (no longer welcomed back in) by two neighborhood bars.

There were times when I wanted to drink less. There were days when I would decide that I was going to drive straight home from work, but then, as I sat behind the wheel, I would watch as my car steered me straight to the beer store. The film "The Exorcist" came out in December of my senior year, and I wondered if I might be possessed by the devil. A lot of the absurdities inside my head were mind games.

One night, I went home drunk and told my mother that I had decided to drink myself to death. The next morning my father said to me, "Dennis, you are too old for me to control you. If you can't control yourself, well—either shape up or get out." That was my bottom. I needed help. I had a cousin whom I knew was in A.A. I went to see him. He was in bed with a hangover. He had left the program and was back to drinking. That evening, we went together to my first A.A. meeting.

REFLECTION 8

Probing the Darkness

I LEARNED TO TELL my story in A.A.. This process influenced the way that I interpret my life. At first it was a straight before and after story. Everything before sobriety was awful, terrible, horrifying. Working on sobriety might be hard, but the overall theme of the beginner's story focuses on how relatively good sober life is when compared with what came before. There's a saying I've often heard at meetings: "My worst day sober is better than my best day drunk."

Over time, it is usual for a recovering alcoholic's story to become less of what we call a bottle story and be much more of a recovery story. It's also true that with time the alcoholic becomes more discriminating when it comes to evaluating their life before sobriety. I discovered that each time I told my story, it came out somewhat differently. I wasn't lying or twisting or even willfully exaggerating. The variations were due to the fact that one's own life story is an extremely complicated thing with so much to say and so many details that one could never tell it exactly one right way. One's own life story is one of the hardest things to interpret, no matter how honest you are.

Compared to many other alcoholics, those who lost their families and their jobs, those who had been in prison or in and out of hospitals, and those with permanent injuries, I have a relatively "high bottom." Having a high bottom has nothing to do with how long your legs are. In A.A., having a high bottom means that when you reached a low point in your life due to your drinking, it perhaps wasn't that bad when compared to the low point of others.

So, I want to go back and re-tell a few things. It is true that by the time I joined A.A. I had no friends, was thrown out by my girlfriend, was flagged at neighborhood bars, and had been told by my father to shape up or get out. Having dwelled so much on the darkness, though, I have to acknowledge that prior to sobriety my life was not all dark every day. I had many sick thoughts, but they were probably mixed in with normal thoughts. With some exceptions, I did well in high school. I had a good family. I was part of a small group of close friends. I had a good long-term, part-time job in a supermarket.

In my early college years, I still had some friends. After a few drinks, I could be rather clever, funny, and crazy in a not always bad way. In 1978, when the movie "Animal House" depicted wild frat parties, one of my old friends said that they must have based the John Belushi character on me. By that time, however, I had been sober for over two years and teaching my own classes as a graduate assistant. I was actually worried about the bad influence that the film might have on my students.

All through college, I managed to hold down my supermarket job by working an all-night twelve-hour shift on Fridays. After a few initial bad semesters, I got mostly good grades. I took Creative Writing and other English courses. I was serious in my study of literature. I wanted to be a writer like Ernest Hemingway (1899–1961)) or F. Scott Fitzgerald (1896–1940) or James Joyce (1882–1941), all of whom had reputations as excessive drinkers. I was terribly sad and confused. I developed an extremely high opinion about my own intellect and my potential as a writer. I remember commenting to a companion that I was becoming dissatisfied with the quality of currently existing literature and that, if I wanted to read literature worthy of the name, I would have to write it myself.

I did notice that many of the literary artists whom I adored tended to be critical of religion and seemed to be agnostic or atheist. Who was I to disagree with these great alcoholic minds? I no longer believed in religion. I took a linguistics course, General Semantics, and became enthralled by the quest for meaning. Maybe there is no God, but there is such a thing as meaning. What is the meaning of life? I also enjoyed the study of European and American Romantic literature. I was especially taken by the Transcendentalism of Ralph Waldo Emerson (1803–1882), who thought that divinity is present in the creative power of human perception and imagination in their interplay with the sacred beauty of nature.[1] I wrote poetry and short stories, and I drank. I received A's on most of my papers for my many English courses, but I was nervous, confused, and unhappy.

When I wrote a philosophy paper on the existence of God in my senior year and expressed some openness to the idea that there is a God, I was influenced by having fallen in love with my girlfriend. I was also impressed by the philosophy teacher who assigned the paper. I remember thinking at the time that this professor was the first practicing Catholic I ever met who was remarkably intelligent. He was remarkably intelligent, for sure, but he was by no means the first brilliant Catholic whom I had met. I was being arrogant by thinking so.

I graduated from college with honors, and I was accepted into an excellent graduate program in English. I took a year off, and then, having gotten sober, went to a different school that offered me substantial financial support.

I have tried to clarify that even in my darkest days there were moments when light would shine through. This more nuanced perspective is appropriate only after one has been in the program for some time. For the newly recovering alcoholic, it is important to tell a simple story that focuses on how bad it was before and how much better it is now. It is not helpful for the new member to start thinking that maybe their prior life wasn't so bad.

There is also the danger of focusing too much and too immediately on underlying issues rather than on the drinking itself. The alcoholic desperately wants to find out that alcohol is not their real problem. They hope that someday, even someday soon, they

---

1. Emerson, "Nature," 231–33.

will be able to drink again. The alcoholic must reject their misconception that alcohol is really their best friend, the only great thing they've got. They need to admit that they are an alcoholic and that drinking has been ruining their life. They need to see how awful their life had become and recognize that alcohol was the main thing dragging them down—*the* problem. Much of that process will begin with Step Four: "[We] made a searching and fearless moral inventory of ourselves."[2]

No one should start working Step Four until they have worked through the first three steps with their sponsor. By that time, many of their underlying issues will start to surface, and these must be addressed. It remains important, though, to deal with one's alcoholism and one's underlying issues in a unified way. Alcoholics need to resist the temptation to think that all they have to do is address their below-the-surface problems, and then they will be free to drink. In some cases, it happens that a person with some alcohol-related problem, such as a single DUI, turns out not to be an alcoholic. In many other cases, though, the reality is that a true alcoholic desperately feels the pull to return to the state of denial.

I have spent this reflection probing the darkness because I want to get my story right. I want to explain the complexities of how an alcoholic's life prior to sobriety was in an important way darkness, and yet from another angle upon broader consideration there will be many ambiguities and often some patches of light. This clarification is especially important to me because, as I tell the story of how God and A.A. brought me out from the darkness and into the light, there had also been many good things in my pre-sober life. When I had an experience of the presence of God (that I will soon tell you about), there were also present in a helpful if subconscious way many positive elements from my prior life. These elements included my family, my religious formation, my overall education, and my experiences of love and friendship— even if at the same time I seemed to be and in important ways was in total darkness.

---

2. *Alcoholics Anonymous*, 59.

REFLECTION 9

My First A.A. Meeting

My cousin took me to my first A.A. meeting. Before I entered the room, I thought that joining A.A. meant that my real life was over. No drinking, no life. I imagined that in A.A. meetings the participants included my cousin plus a bunch of extremely old men sitting around in wife-beater tee-shirts playing checkers.

As we walked in, I saw a variety of men and women of various ages, many of whom were smoking cigarettes and drinking coffee as they chatted with each other. The people seemed like they felt at home. No one was wearing a wife-beater tee-shirt or playing checkers.

The meeting was in a big rectangular room in a small building that used to be a police lodge. Three pairs of rectangular tables were arranged to form one long table with a chair placed in every possible spot. I estimate that about twenty people could sit around it, with seats for another twenty or so around the perimeter. There were three meetings a day held in that room every day of the week. The one my cousin took me to was the 8:30 evening meeting.

A few things about that meeting stick out in my mind. Everyone was friendly and said supportive, reassuring things. The person leading the meeting had various members read from short texts. One text, from the Big Book, was called "How It Works."[1] It

---

1. *Alcoholics Anonymous*, 58–60.

MY FIRST A.A. MEETING

starts out, "Rarely have we seen a person fail who has thoroughly followed our path." What a message of hope! The passage went on to stress the importance of honesty several times. Those who don't recover are "constitutionally incapable of being honest with themselves." The A.A. program "demands rigorous honesty." Many people with mental or emotional disorders "can and do recover if they have the capacity to be honest."

That reading would be recited at the beginning of every meeting. I attended almost ninety meetings in my first ninety days, and I was deeply struck by those words from the moment I first heard them. From the earliest time in my recovery, the connection between honesty and sobriety got through to me deeply.

On that first night, a man of about thirty was celebrating the first anniversary of his sobriety. Much of the conversation centered around giving him praise and encouragement. Someone even brought a cake with a single candle. I was impressed by the fact that this man who looked happy and healthy had the same problem that I did and yet had not taken a drink in an entire year. This accomplishment was mind-blowing. Here was the evidence sitting right in front of me that long-term sobriety is possible.

I recognized a dual message. Along with "this can be done" was the point, "this is hard." Sobriety is possible, but not easy to attain. It is possible if you can completely give yourself to this simple program and if you have the capacity to be honest.

The alcoholic at their first meeting has plenty of reason to doubt their chances of success. In my case, I was a compulsive drinker. My drinking didn't seem to have all that much to do with choice. I experienced myself as someone who had to drink as well as someone who had to keep drinking once I started. As I lost friends and became more and more of a mess, it seemed that drinking was the only thing I enjoyed. I loved to drink. Drinking was everything to me. It would be hard to imagine going a week or two without a drink. How could I possibly make it a whole year without one?

A.A. has a powerful tool to deal with that particular problem. It's called "One Day at a Time." You don't have to tell yourself that you are quitting drinking for the rest of your life or for a year or even for a week. You are just not going to drink today. You can remember plenty of times when you went a day without a drink. You know you can make it through one day, even if there may be moments when you will have to think in terms of hours or minutes. If you can't think in terms of quitting for a year, you can quit for one day, and those days can add up. If you string enough "one days" back-to-back, eventually they can add up to a whole year or even more.

Yet you are likely to go through days when you want a drink badly. This is why you need to learn to make use of the various tools of the program. Call your sponsor. Go to a meeting. Read the Big Book. Think that drink through—where is it going to take you? Work the steps. Say a prayer. Do something to help another alcoholic.

Of all the things that surprised me at my first meeting, I observed one thing that really shocked me. It was my previous experience that if there was to be any lively conversation among a group of adults, alcohol had to be a part of it. For free-flowing communication to take place, the liquor also had to be free-flowing. In my case, I could have a chat with one person over a cup of coffee if it was during the day. Beyond that, I needed to drink to be able to talk with people. I thought that any conversation of any length had to take place in a bar. I was astonished to find a group of thirty or so sober people sitting around a room having conversations about serious things while at the same time relaxing, joking, and having fun. I could say to myself what Hamlet said to Horatio: "There are more things in heaven and earth, Horatio, than are dreamt of in your philosophy."[2]

---

2. Shakespeare, *Hamlet*, Act I, scene 5.

REFLECTION 10

Touched by God's Presence

I HAD A LIFE-CHANGING experience of God when I was in a rehabilitation center for alcoholics. Before I try to express what it was, I'll need to explain a few things in order to set the scene.

Earlier I mentioned the philosophy professor who had me write a paper on the existence of God. He would become a lifelong mentor to me. He would also be an important part of my life-changing experience.

During my first week of sobriety, I was making the 8:30 evening meeting and then going into work at my supermarket job at 11:00 p.m. I think that perhaps I didn't look so good, like maybe I looked unhealthy and in need of some serious help. On a weekend day, a couple of people I had met at the police lodge meetings took me to a rehabilitation center north of my city. We attended a meeting there, and they showed me around. At the time, I didn't get the impression that they were suggesting to me that I enter the rehab program. They went to that meeting regularly, and, as far as I knew, they were just bringing me along. In retrospect, I think that planting the idea of the rehab in my head was a big part of their motivation in inviting me.

I had a lot of issues that I needed address. As an adult, I was diagnosed with an anxiety disorder. This condition is not uncommon among alcoholics. I've also been diagnosed with ADHD. Frankly, there have been periods of my life when I could pass for being manic-depressive or having obsessive-compulsive disorder. I could name other potential diagnoses. I think that my biggest personality issue in the earliest days of my recovery was that I was an egomaniac who lacked a coherent worldview.

During the eighth night of my sobriety, I worked through the night. I was having paranoid obsessive thoughts about something related to my former girlfriend. In any case, I tried to call her all night, but her phone was busy. I imagined that certain things were happening, and I was freaking out. I manufactured a bizarre story in my mind about where she was and what she was doing and even called someplace in a different city trying to reach her. When I left work at 7:00 a.m., I raced over to her apartment, and we discovered that her phone was off the hook.

I was in a state of desperation, although I tried to hide my condition from her. I then drove to the rehab center and told someone there that I was having a mental breakdown. I was admitted to a twenty-eight-day residential recovery program. My insurance through work would pay for it. I went home to pack some things and tell my parents. They were supportive. I began the program that afternoon.

Entering the rehab was a total humiliation for me. The college English major who was going to be a great writer met up with his mirror low self-image. I have come to believe that it is usually the case that an inflated ego and a low self-image go hand in hand.

My stay lasted exactly four weeks. Mostly everything was done communally in groups, though you did receive a small amount of one-on-one counseling. Every day you ate three meals together with everyone. On the weekdays, you spent some time on your chores, three hours in group therapy, and a couple of hours reading the Big Book and other A.A. literature as well as working on your own program individually. There were also lectures and some A.A. meetings which outsiders would attend. The weekends had some A.A. meetings but were lighter in schedule. Visitors were welcome.

Your main job in rehab was to work the first four steps of A.A. I've already mentioned that the first three have to do with a basic reorientation of one's life. You admit that you have a problem. You come to believe that a power greater than yourself can restore you to sanity. You then give your will and your life over to the care of God *as you understand Him.*

Step Four reads, "[We] made a searching and fearless inventory of ourselves."[1] The Big Book lays out how to do Step Four, but I tackled it ambitiously and compulsively by writing what was basically a sixty-page autobiography in which I was very harsh on myself. I have often heard in meetings since then that a Step Four should be honest and thorough but also balanced. Not everything about you has been bad. My own inventory represented one of those times when my honesty went beyond truth to scrupulosity. It was anything but balanced.

This inventory did help me, though, by making me realize that I really am an alcoholic. Without writing anything down, an alcoholic can feed denial by dismissing each outrageous incident as they occur as maybe being bad but not representative of an overall problem. When I actually wrote about many of the times that alcohol got me into trouble, a pattern emerged that was impossible for me to deny. Later, after a few months of sobriety, I would find a way to reembrace denial and then drink again. When I was writing my inventory, though, the obvious truth that I had been hiding from myself came out into the clear.

There are places in the Big Book that suggest that the only hope for an alcoholic lies in the possibility of having a spiritual experience. The renowned Swiss psychiatrist Carl Jung (1875–1961) offered a similar opinion.[2] Bill Wilson, the co-founder of A.A., had such a spiritual experience. He was in a hotel room, and, in a moment of prayer, it was as if a bright light filled the room. Other members testify to having had a spiritual experience. Step Twelve begins, "Having had a spiritual awakening as a result of these steps . . . ." And yet there are also other passages that explain that not every recovering alcoholic has a dramatic spiritual experience, but rather spiritual experience can happen gradually over time.

1. *Alcoholics Anonymous,* 59.
2. "The Bill W.–Carl Jung Letters," *The AA Grapevine,* 1963.

I had read about what Carl Jung said and about what happened to Bill Wilson. I was also a person who had been formed in Catholic faith, even if I was in denial about my faith as deeply as I was in denial about my alcoholism. Somehow, when I was in the rehab, the suggestion got through to me that I should try to pray.

I went up to my room, which I shared with three other patients. There was no one there at that moment. I started to pray for the first time in many years. I felt that I was in the presence of God, and I felt that God loved me. I felt it inside myself.

In my mind appeared the image of the face of my philosophy professor, smiling. I did not for a moment think that my teacher was God or anything like that. Actually, I worry that that detail might be confusing, and the only reason that I include it is because that is how it happened.

I felt the presence of God, and I felt that God loved me. My life changed at that moment. My life would never be the same—even though a couple of months later I would drink again—for most of a summer—before I made it back to A.A. and recovery. Still, what happened in that moment altered my life forever.

PART THREE

A Ninety Day Wonder Grows
Rapidly Then Relapses

REFLECTION 11

Was It Really God Who Became Present to Me?

AT THE END OF the previous reflection, I told of how I felt the presence of God and also felt loved by God. I did not raise questions or offer cautious qualifications about the experience.

I did make an effort to set the experience in a context. It wasn't as if I was walking along a beach on a sunny day and was suddenly struck by lightning. My encounter with God happened when I was a patient in a rehab center. It happened at a time when I was suffering a great humiliation. It happened after reading that having a spiritual experience represented my best shot at dealing with my alcoholism. It happened after reading the stories of Bill Wilson and others who had such an experience. It happened when I took the suggestion to pray after having not prayed for many years. And so, even though at the time my experience seemed to be immediate and direct, I was acknowledging that it was not purely unconditioned.

Over time, a nagging question would arise for me about what happened. Was it truly an experience of God, or was it merely psychological? I can't say that the question was personally troubling for me. I treasured the experience. It was more about how to express what happened to me to the few people whom I would tell about it. What is it that I am talking about? What kind of claim am I making?

I gradually concluded that my experience could probably be explained satisfactorily to some people in purely psychological terms. I do admit that my encounter with God was something that took place in my mind, in the deepest part of my psyche. I didn't levitate or sprout a halo above my head. My encounter occurred on the level of thought, imagination, and feeling. To someone who did not believe in God, it might seem that my experience of feeling loved was perhaps positive, but only real to the extent that it was something that happened within my own head and nowhere else.

For me personally, though, a purely psychological explanation was not at all satisfactory. I had already taken Step Two by which I came to believe that a power greater than myself could restore me to sanity. By definition, a power greater than myself is something that exists beyond my own mind. My point of contact might be within my own head, but I was encountering something or rather Someone who was greater than myself. I can acknowledge that the experience was deeply psychological, but it is not enough for me to say that it was merely psychological.

Years later I would read in *St. Joan*, a play by George Bernard Shaw (1856–1950), a scene that would speak deeply to my belief that my spiritual experience was more than subjective. When the aristocrat Robert de Baudricourt questions Joan of Arc about the source of her visions, she claims that they come from God. De Baudricourt replies that they come from her imagination. Joan of Arc's retort is that the messages of God come to us through our imagination.[1]

De Baudricourt is offering an interpretation of Joan's visions that I would classify as reductionist. He reduces Joan's experience to the workings of her mind. Joan, in contrast, acknowledges the role of her mind in her spiritual experience of God, but she does not confine it to that.

Even though I did have a transformative experience that took place in a moment, the spiritual awakening that I had through working the A.A. program can be better understood as something that developed gradually over time. Many recovering alcoholics

---

1. Shaw, *Saint Joan*, scene 1.

cannot point to one big bang moment when they see a flash of light. I have heard it said in meetings that one should neither pursue nor expect such a moment, even though quite a number of members can testify to one.

My experience of the presence and love of God did not immediately take away my desire to drink. I remained haunted by a compulsion to drink throughout the first year of my sobriety. My experience did not immediately make me mature. It did not take away from the importance of working the A.A. program on a daily basis. It did not make my recovery easy, though it probably made it more possible and less hard than it would have been otherwise. My experience did not prevent me from later drinking for a period of almost two months before I made it back into the A.A. program.

Yet, my encounter with God was profoundly life-changing in both the short term and long term. When I was drinking, I woke up every morning into a world that made no sense. As someone now aware of being loved by God, I woke up into a world that had been created for a purpose. I did not know exactly what the meaning of life was, but I became convinced that there was one. I could feel its texture within the deepest level of my being.

I was no longer the center of my own universe. I now lived in a reality in which God was at the center. A burden was lifted from me. I didn't have to carry the weight of the world on my shoulders. God is a good God. Here I was, a broken-down alcoholic at the lowest point in my life, yet God loved me.

Living in God's world gave me a sense of spiritual equality with other people. I came to the realization that, even if there were some special and even unique qualities about me that God loved, the deepest reason God loved me was the same as the reason God loved everyone else. I felt that affirming God's love for me and affirming God's love for everyone went hand in hand. To deny one would require a denial of the other.

I connected this insight with a teaching from my grade school catechism as well as from readings at Mass. I quote the version from Mark:

> One of the scribes came near and heard them disputing with one another, and seeing that he answered them well, he asked him, "Which commandment is the first of all?" Jesus answered, "The first is, 'Hear, O Israel: the Lord our God, the Lord is one; you shall love the Lord your God with all your heart, and with all your soul, and with all your mind, and with all your strength.' The second is this, 'You shall love your neighbor as yourself.' There is no other commandment greater than these" (Mark 12: 28–31).

I saw in this teaching a spiritual truth, that love of God, love of neighbor, and love of self all go together. You can't do any of them right without doing all three at once.

My encounter with God has proved itself to be fruitful over the long term. I still look back to it as a before and after moment. Yes, I would drink again. I believe, though, that as a result of my experience, I went from being a certifiable egomaniac to being a person who can usually recognize when ego-inflation starts to flare up and who has tools to stamp it down. Six months later, I was given the gift of sobriety which I have maintained through the grace of God and A.A. for nearly five decades. I would return to the Catholic faith in which I had been formed in my youth. I would pursue my interest in religious questions and earn a doctorate in religious studies. I would have a long and fruitful career as a professor in a Catholic university, teaching and writing about Catholic theology. I would marry, and my wife and I would have several children and grandchildren, none of whom have ever seen me under the influence of alcohol.

By God and A.A., I was carried forth out of the darkness and into the light.

REFLECTION 12

Are There Just Two Kinds of People in the World?

THE AMERICAN PHILOSOPHER AND psychologist William James (1842–1910), in his 1902 book, *The Varieties of Religious Experience*, claimed that when it came to religion, there are basically two kinds of people: the healthy-souled and the sick-souled.[1] The healthy-souled are normal, regular people of basically good character who are not in need of a radical makeover. The sick-souled, in contrast, are those in need of a dramatic turn-about to bring them out of darkness into light. They are people who live with extreme fear, anxiety, self-loathing, and mistrust. They wrestle with evil, yet they are also the ones who can be liberated by a sudden transformation. They are people like St. Paul, St. Augustine, and Martin Luther, people with dark or burdensome pasts who become leading beacons of light.

The healthy-souled make up by far the majority of the population. Such a person might attend church, but, according to James, they are not the primary subject matter of religion. Religion is all about the sick-souled people. It's about the battle between good and evil.

The North African bishop and writer St. Augustine (354–430 CE) shows an awareness of the basic concept underlying James'

1. James, *Varieties*, 125–162.

distinction in his *Confessions*, in a passage he directly addresses to God:

> If there is anyone whom you have called, who by responding to your summons has avoided these sins which he finds me remembering and confessing in my own life as he reads this, let him not mock me; for I have been healed by the same doctor who has granted him the grace not to fall ill, or at least to fall ill less seriously. Let such a person, therefore, love you just as much, or even more, on seeing that the same physician who rescued me from sinful diseases of such gravity has kept him immune.[2]

If I may anachronistically project James' categories into the above passage, I can say that Augustine identifies himself as a sick-souled person saved by God. He wants healthy-souled people not to look down on him but to realize that the same God who saved him is the God who prevented them from ever becoming so bad. The healthy-souled should love God as much or even more than does Augustine for that reason, and should think: there but for the grace of God go I.

Bill Wilson read *The Varieties of Religious Experience* sometime after he had his own dramatic experience.[3] The book helped him to realize that what happened to him was not something crazy. James' finding that a religious experience is often preceded by some kind of humbling had some influence on the formulation of the first three steps. In later years, Wilson would refer to James, who died in 1910, long before the founding of A.A., as one of the founders.

I was just a few years sober when I first read *The Varieties of Religious Experience*. I identified right away with James' description of the sick-souled. That was me. I may have even felt more than a tinge of pride in being able to place myself in the same group as Paul, Augustine, and Luther.

To this day, I still find the categories of healthy-souled and sick-souled to have some explanatory power, even though binary

---

2. Augustine, *Confessions*, 41 (II, 7, 15).
3. "The Bill W.–Carl Jung Letters," *The AA Grapevine*, Jan. 1963.

classifications have their limits. If, from one point of view, one can place people into one of two categories, there is usually another point of view from which people might be placed somewhere across a broad spectrum. In many cases when one can rightfully describe a difference in kind, one can also take another angle and talk about a difference in degree. Not everyone fits easily into one of two well-defined categories. Even those who do fit do not like to be stereotyped.

I kind of like the idea that I am a sick-souled person. Around my seventh year of sobriety, I was teaching an English course, The Bible as Literature, in a college program in a prison where the students were serving long-term sentences. One day we were covering the novel by the English writer Thomas Hardy (1840–1928), *The Mayor of Casterbridge*, some of which is based on the stories of Saul and David in 1 Samuel. Saul is dark, sad, suspicious, and brooding. David is light-hearted and golden. At the end of class, one of the students approached me. He wagged his finger at me and said, "You're Saul!" I was quite stunned by this, though not in a negative way. I found it remarkable that the man was able to look inside of me so deeply and accurately.

Being sick-souled, however, does not completely define me. I did have an experience of being brought out of the darkness into the light, but it is just as true that my overall spiritual awakening in A.A. took place gradually and required a lot of effort.

The English lay Catholic theologian Rosemary Haughton (1927–2024), in her book, *The Transformation of Man*, makes a distinction that can be compared with the one made by James. She points out that both Protestants and Catholics talk about *conversion*. Protestants, however, have tended more to stress *transformation*, whereas Catholics have tended to stress *formation*. Haughton argues that conversion properly understood should include both formation and transformation.[4]

Haughton's distinction helps explain the Catholic ambivalence toward John Newton's 1779 hymn, "Amazing Grace." When I was a child, this hymn was considered to be strictly for

---

4. Haughton, *The Transformation of Man*, 6–12.

Protestants. The famous opening lines are: "Amazing grace, how sweet the sound/That saved a wretch like me!" The implication that all human beings are wretches apart from the intervention of God's grace reflected an understanding of the human person that was too negative for Catholics. Sometime in the second half of the twentieth century, the hymn began to appear in Catholic hymnals, but with a meaningful change made by a United Reform Church minister and hymn-writer, Brian Wren (b. 1936). In place of the phrase, "that saved a wretch like me," were the words, "that saved and set me free."

Nowadays, out of respect for ecumenism and historical accuracy, most Catholic hymnals contain Newton's original version. It took a while, though, because Catholics are not used to stressing how we are undeserving wretches who need to be snatched out of the darkness. Catholics acknowledge sin while giving more stress to goodness. We connect the idea of spiritual growth with Baptism followed by a Catholic education focusing on faith, sacraments, and morality. We have tended to shy away from the concept of being "born-again" through a dramatic experience of conversion.

The distinction between transformation and formation has helped me to question James' claim that religion is all about the sick-souled. A bit like A.A., James was not allied with any particular sect or denomination. When it came to thinking about what religion is, however, he leaned toward Protestantism. In contrast to James, perhaps because of my Catholic bias, in my judgment religion has as much to do with the healthy-souled as with the sick-souled.

I also wonder whether in addition to putting people into James' binary categories, it is also important to consider how various cases can be spread out across a continuum. Perhaps there are ways in which some people are both a bit sick-souled and a bit healthy-souled, in need of some degree of both transformation and formation.

Many A.A. members, though not all, fit pretty easily into the sick-souled category. Most recovering alcoholics can identify with moving from darkness into light, but not all have some identifiable moment of spiritual transformation. Even those of us who did have such a moment have to keep working gradually to attain the formation that can help our transformation be much more than just one instant.

REFLECTION 13

Reading the Gospels

IN LATE MARCH 1975, after twenty-eight days in rehab, I returned to live with my parents and went back to my all-night supermarket job. The person I am still referring to as my girlfriend was back in my life, though it would be a while before we would be a couple again. She was relieved that I was doing something about my problem. I changed my education goals from studying English in graduate school (and eventually becoming one of the great authors) to earning a certificate to teach English in high school. I enrolled in a program in summer 1975 which set me on a trajectory to get my teaching certificate by May 1976.

On some level, I always wanted to be a high school English teacher. I didn't pursue a teaching certificate in college because I was deathly afraid of speaking in front of a classroom or to a group of any size. How I overcame that obstacle will be a topic for another reflection.

I spent my time that spring mostly working, going to many A.A. meetings, and reading the four gospels. I read them with the specific intention of trying to figure out if I thought there was any truth to Christianity. I was especially interested in what would be said about the divinity of Jesus. This exploration was a part of my A.A. search for the God of my understanding. I used our family's Bible, which was a red-letter edition, meaning that all words that were attributed to Jesus were printed in red.

I examined the gospels very attentively, though I did not interpret them as if they were exact news reports. It seemed obvious to me that there were different genres of writing and many levels of meaning at work. Much of what I read I had heard before, even many times, whether in religion classes or in church. I had never, though, read the gospels all the way through with any sense of continuity or context. Many, many questions formed in my mind, questions that I would pursue in my later studies.

I was deeply moved by my intense reading of the gospels. There are things that struck me at the time that I have remembered ever since. There's a scene in the 1956 film *The Ten Commandments* in which the finger of God writes the commandments on stone tablets with fire. I make this reference not because anything exactly like that literally happened to me, but because I do feel as though certain elements of the gospels were emblazoned in my consciousness with lifelong effects.

At that time, I still had questions about the divinity of Jesus. Matthew, Mark, and Luke, known together as the synoptic gospels, display certain ambiguities surrounding this issue. Especially in the Gospel of Mark, Jesus is very reluctant in public to say anything about his own divinity. Jesus more often called himself the Son of Man. The story of Jesus' Baptism in Mark reads as though Jesus himself is having a transformative religious experience. The wording seems to stress the subjective nature of the event:

> And just as he was coming up out of the water, he saw the heavens torn apart and the Spirit descending like a dove on him. And a voice came from heaven, "You are my Son, the Beloved; with you I am well pleased" (Mark 1:10–11).

Did Jesus have an experience like Bill Wilson had? Like I had? Yet even in these synoptic gospels, there were claims about Jesus being the Messiah and the son of God. There seemed to be a back-and-forth tension over the issue. In the Gospel of John, though, which was written later than the synoptic gospels, the claims made about Jesus as well as those attributed to Jesus himself were much stronger and unambiguous. I felt apprehensive, a bit like, "Oh boy, here we go."

There are many points held in tension in the gospels. For example, in Matthew 12:30a, Jesus says, "Whoever is not with me is against me." In Mark 9:40, Jesus says, "Whoever is not against us is for us." Did Jesus say both of these things? Could be. As a person who was averaging at least one A.A. meeting per day at the time, however, what I heard was a back-and-forth dialogue taking place among people who were quoting Jesus. It was as if there was a group conversation going on in the background of each gospel. It wasn't a matter of contradictions but more a matter of points that need to be held in a dynamic tension.

You often encounter points held in tension in A.A. meetings. For example, you might hear one person say, "Stay away from people, places, and things that are associated with alcohol." In the same meeting, another person might say, "If you have a good reason, you can go anywhere and stay sober." These points are not contradictory, but they do seem to work together as points to be held in tension. The first person might be saying that, if you want to get sober, you can't just go back and hang out with your old drinking buddies in bars like you used to. The other person might be saying that if you need to go to a wedding, or maybe to a business event that is held in a bar, you can do it. If you are fairly new in the program, you just need to prepare yourself for it, and you can make it through.

The gospels gave me the impression that there were some parallels between Christianity in the first century and A.A. in the twentieth century. Something powerful was erupting through the creation of rapidly spreading communities. In contrast to the hopelessness and desperation of my drinking life, I was experiencing A.A. as a wonderful, miraculous remedy sent directly by a loving and merciful God. I sensed that there was something deeply analogous going on in Christianity during the times when the gospels were being written. In both cases, the spiritual momentum seemed unstoppable.

REFLECTION 14

Seeking the Will of God

STEPS TWO AND THREE put me in connection with the God of my understanding. Step Eleven says, "[We] sought through prayer and meditation to improve our conscious contact with God *as we understood Him*, praying only for knowledge of His will for us and the power to carry that out."[1]

I took more than a little notice when, in the Gospel of Mark, Jesus walks in the Garden of Gethsemane: "And going a little farther, he threw himself on the ground and prayed that, if it were possible, the hour might pass from him. He said, 'Abba, Father, for you all things are possible; remove this cup from me; yet, not what I want, but what you want'" (Mark 14:35–36). Similar words are found in Matthew. In Luke, the parallel passage reads, "Father, if you are willing, remove this cup from me; yet, not my will but yours be done" (Luke 22:42). So, Jesus himself, when deciding to go through with his impending torture and death, is aware of a difference between his own will and the will of his Father. Jesus himself is someone who seeks the will of God and then carries it out.

The story of the Annunciation in the first chapter of Luke is also about accepting and doing the will of God. When the angel Gabriel announces to Mary that God wills for her to conceive a child who will be called the Son of the Most High, she responds,

---

1. *Alcoholics Anonymous*, 59.

"Here am I, the servant of the Lord; let it be with me according to your word" (Luke 1:38). So, the great happening of God becoming a human being included another human being attaining knowledge of God's will and agreeing to carry it out.

But how does a regular person find out the will of God? I didn't expect that an angel would appear to me. In the story of Jesus in the garden as well as in many other places in the gospels, Jesus discerned the will of God through prayer. That path seemed do-able. It was also compatible with the phrasing of Step Eleven that encourages prayer and meditation as the means for improving our conscious contact with God. But were there any other clues for discerning God's will?

For this question, I found it helpful to pay attention to what Jesus said about commandments. In one story (Matt 19:16–26), a rich young man asks Jesus what good deed he must do to merit eternal life. Jesus replies that he should keep the commandments. And so, it was evident that keeping the commandments is a way of doing God's will. But then the rich young man says that he has kept the commandments, and so "what more do I lack?" Jesus tells him to sell what he has, give the money to the poor, and to follow him. Jesus had not given that response as his first answer, and so perhaps not everyone is called to such a radical form of discipleship. But some form of following Jesus did appear to be a good way of carrying out God's will.

The rich young man chooses not to follow Jesus and instead sadly walks away. Jesus tells the disciples that "it is easier for a camel to go through the eye of a needle than for someone who is rich to enter the kingdom of God." When the astounded disciples ask Jesus, "Then who can be saved?" Jesus responds, "For mortals it is impossible, but for God all things are possible." To someone who had shown up at the doors of A.A. feeling hopeless, that last line felt like a lifesaver in a storm-tossed sea. It was something to grasp onto and hold tight. What seemed impossible to me is possible for God.

My A.A. experience put me in touch with yet another way to seek God's will: consult with people whom you trust. Bring up

SEEKING THE WILL OF GOD

your need for direction in a meeting. Talk it over with your sponsor. Seek help from people who have special knowledge or training regarding your particular situation.

In my later studies, I would learn that Thomas Aquinas taught that, when it comes to particular choices, we do not actually know the will of God in a specific manner. We can, however, seek to discern and to do what is truly good. By trying to do what is good, we are conforming our will with the will of God.[2]

Jesus had more things to say about commandments. When asked what the greatest commandment is, he replied, "You shall love the Lord your God with all your heart, and with all your soul, and with all your mind. This is the greatest and first commandment. And a second is like it: You shall love your neighbor as yourself. On these two commandments hang all the law and the prophets" (Matt 22:34–40). In his final speech to the disciples after the Last Supper in the Gospel of John, Jesus says, "This is my commandment, that you love one another as I have loved you" (John 15:12).

That last line made me profoundly happy. Jesus didn't say, "Build me a great monument that looks a bit like the Sphynx but with my face on it." No, he commanded his disciples to love one another. You would think that if someone commands you to do something, it will be something that you otherwise would not want to do. This commandment of love, though, expressed what we all would really want to do if we thought about it deeply enough.

The Catholic spiritual writer Richard Rohr (b. 1943) points out that seeking the will of God in prayer can "help you to know what you really desire."[3] In other words, as you grow spiritually, your own will and the will of God grow closer together. What God wants for you and what you truly desire start to align.

By reading the gospels, I was able to see that the element of spirituality in A.A. that was so deeply connected with and even defined by seeking and doing the will of God was also a key, integral element of the gospel message at the very core of Christianity.

2. Aquinas, *Summa Theologiae,* II, 19, 10.
3. Rohr, *Breathing,* 96.

In my mind, Christianity and A.A. could now be experienced as fundamentally compatible.

I stress the personal element of this connection because I am not trying in these reflections to persuade recovering alcoholics to become Christian or Catholic or necessarily to join any religion at all. Later, when I studied religion in graduate school, I saw that a similar link can also be made between A.A. and other religions. The Hebrew story of Abraham and Isaac is all about the willingness to do what God wants. The very word, "Islam," translates as surrender or submission, and what is submitted to above all is the will of God. Keven Griffin (b. 1950), a Buddhist who regularly gives Twelve Step retreats, equates the giving over of one's will and life in Step Three with the eight-fold path, especially with Right Intention.[4]

As a scholar of religion, I have come to think that it is wrong either to declare that all religions are basically the same or to deny that there exist deep similarities among them. There are important and meaningful differences, but there are also deep similarities. I am a believing Catholic who struggles to live with intellectual integrity in a pluralistic world. My A.A. experiences have helped me to do that. I respect other religions and worldviews and try not to make assumptions about their ultimate status. Divine revelation does not give much direct information on this topic. The plurality of religions represents to me a great mystery.

Although I still had many questions, I came away from my reading of the gospels convinced that Christianity itself was so powerful and amazing that it wasn't just something that human beings invented on their own. There was something other-worldly about it, something transcendent. I thought that Christianity, even if it contained many human elements, ultimately comes from God.

In the seventies, there was a commercial on television for cold medicine capsules that contained "tiny time pills." I remember thinking that the gospels were full of something like tiny time pills that would continue to explode in my brain indefinitely in a most positive way. I decided that I was a Christian. I believed in

---

4. Griffin, *One Breath*, 57–61.

the God that Jesus Christ talked about and with whom he related. I believed in the Ten Commandments and in the two greatest commandments of loving God and loving neighbor. I wanted to seek and do the will of God. And I did come to believe in the divinity (along with the humanity) of Jesus.

REFLECTION 15

Diving Back into Drinking and Denial

New members in A.A. are recommended to make ninety meetings in ninety days. The basic idea is to give the newly recovering alcoholic a solid foundation by immersing them in the world of A.A. I spent twenty-eight of my first ninety days in the rehab where we had several A.A. meetings each week. After rehab, I often went to more than one meeting per day. I came in just under the ninety meetings in ninety days goal.

A related phrase is "the ninety-day wonder." This label describes with humorous but still pointed sarcasm a person with just a few months of sobriety who appears to have become a know-it-all who doesn't need to listen anymore.

I was a ninety-day wonder. I had improved dramatically both physically and mentally. Having gone from darkness into light, I became happier than I had perhaps ever been. Between attending so many A.A. meetings and reading the gospels, I had a new sense of meaning and purpose in life.

I still struggled with a strong craving, at times even a compulsion, to drink. This desire to drink has a powerful influence on the mind of the alcoholic. The drives that had compelled me for many years were not going to go away easily. If I was going to make it, I had to use daily the tools of the program, such as the meetings, my sponsor, the steps, the Big Book, the telephone, and prayer. I also had to rely on slogans like "One Day at a Time" and "Think That Drink Through." I especially had to depend upon a power greater than myself because there was no way that I could stay sober by my own strength.

The great majority of newly recovering alcoholics want to drink. They want it badly. I know I did. I would catch myself fantasizing about it. It was a good thing that I could call somebody or else go to a meeting.

My parents, now long deceased, were Irish Americans for whom drinking was an important part of their culture and everyday life. One evening they told me that they were proud of me, but they wished I could just be normal again. They said that it was great that I had taken care of my problem, but they didn't want to see me suffer about it my whole life. In other words, they were encouraging me to drink. In 1975, there was more stigma attached to alcoholism than there is today. Maybe it was partly for themselves that they said this because they didn't want their son to be an oddball. I think, though, that it was probably more out of care for me. They didn't want to see me have to go through life as a teetotaler just because I had had some control issues.

My girlfriend independently said similar things. She thought that now that I learned not to drink like a wild hog, it would be a shame not to be able to just enjoy a few drinks. She herself hardly drank. She would occasionally have a glass of wine with dinner. Whether it was more for her sake or for my sake I don't know, but she wanted me to be normal.

I do not at all blame my parents or my girlfriend for encouraging me to drink. Many people have a hard time accepting that anyone whom they know personally could be an actual alcoholic. Their thinking goes something like this: Real alcoholics are the people who live on Skid Row. For regular people, an addiction is simply a bad habit, not a disease. Habits are just a matter of self-control. Maybe there's not really such a thing as alcoholism. Or maybe you could call it a syndrome, but not a disease. The disease model may work practically speaking to relieve guilt and to set the habitual drunk on the road to recovery, but it is more of a tool than an objective reality.

As someone who desperately wanted to drink, that type of thinking appealed to me. I couldn't be an alcoholic because there's really no such thing as alcoholism. I had a bad problem, but I had taken care of it.

Perhaps I had legitimate reasons to wonder whether I was truly an alcoholic. Writing out my Fourth Step in the rehab brought me out of my denial by revealing a long and consistent pattern of problem drinking, often with terrible hangovers and other severe consequences such as the loss of friends or a night in jail. Now, however, I was a ninety-day wonder with good health and a newly acquired spirituality, and perhaps I would be able to drink moderately. There is even a passage in the Big Book that reads:

> We do not like to pronounce an individual as alcoholic, but you can quickly diagnose yourself. Step over to the nearest barroom and try some controlled drinking. Try to drink and stop abruptly. Try it more than once. It will not take long for you to decide if you are honest with yourself about it. It may be worth a bad case of jitters if you get a full knowledge of your condition.[1]

In A.A. meetings that strategy is referred to, sometimes with a hint of humorous sarcasm, as "experimenting."

It was July 4th weekend when, with a little over four months of sobriety, I went out with my girlfriend and another friend of hers. I drank four cans of beer. That was fine; I didn't need to drink any more. The next night I was by myself and drank six cans of beer. Nothing to it. The following day, I got completely plastered out of my mind. After that, I continued to keep busy with school and work, but I stopped going to A.A. meetings and drank on and off for close to two months. I do not remember how many times or how much.

I continued to think of myself as a spiritual person who tried not only to follow the commandments but also to love God and

---

1. *Alcoholics Anonymous*, 31–32.

DIVING BACK INTO DRINKING AND DENIAL

other people. Once I started to drink again, however, I was back into denial about my problem. As an active alcoholic, I arranged my whole life, including my patterns of thought, around my drinking. A great rationalizer replaced the rational operator of my brain.

As I continued to pursue my high school teaching certificate, I ran into one of my former professors on campus one day. He was somebody I had a lot of respect for. He asked how I was doing, and I told him that I had been through a rehab but was now drinking occasionally. He said that he knew people who had that problem who found that the best way to deal with it was not to drink again for the rest of their life. He planted a seed that was to have a big influence on me.

About the third week of August, I shared a room at a seashore resort with an old friend of mine. I don't recall much of what happened. I went on a binge for several days. My friend was disgusted with me.

I do remember being in the room by myself on the morning of our last day in the motel. I was lying by the toilet and throwing up frequently. I had a headache so bad that I thought I was dying. I had not prayed for a couple of months. I promised God that if I lived I would go to confession. There's more to this story, which I will pick up in the next reflection. I do want to mention, however, that I have not had a drink since that day, now approaching fifty years.

PART FOUR

Making My Way Back Both to A.A. and the Catholic Church

REFLECTION 16

Confession Followed by an A.A. Meeting

THROUGHOUT THESE REFLECTIONS, I am trying to come as close as possible to being completely honest. I know, though, that I am not always being absolutely accurate. Memories of individual incidents can tend to be off a bit. When you string your memories together into a narrative, you are engaging in a process of selective reconstruction.

I count August 25, 1975 as the first day of my continuous sobriety. I'm not sure if that was the day that I promised God that I would go to confession or the day after that. I'm not exactly sure if I have the date right at all.

That promise to God came from somewhere out of the depths of my being. I don't really know what was going on in my mind at the time. In retrospect, I don't think that I was really physically close to death when I made that pledge, but psychologically, it was a near-death experience. Thinking that your own death is imminent can open up some doors in your mind.

From when I read the gospels until I made that promise, I had started to regard myself as a Christian but had not consciously been considering going back to the Catholic Church. I suspected, however, that alcohol was not my real problem. The underlying problem was sin. I was haunted by sin and guilt. For someone who was brought up intensely Catholic, there was a remedy for that. When I was a child, it was called the Sacrament of Penance. It has since been re-christened the Sacrament of Reconciliation, though people often still just say "confession."

Step Five in A.A. has elements that overlap with confession: "[We] admitted to God, to ourselves, and to another human being the exact nature of our wrongs."[1] In fact, when I first got sober, it was common for Catholic alcoholics to take their Fifth Step with a priest, usually a priest who was himself in A.A. I had formally taken the first four steps when I was in the rehab. I found a sponsor a few weeks later, but I had not yet taken my Fifth Step.

According to my journal entry, I kept my promise to God and went to confession on Friday, August 29, 1975. Now that's a fact. Presumably, I was about five days sober, and so I count August 25 as my first day of sobriety.

Behind the Catholic high school that I attended was the rectory where the priests who taught there lived. The priests had said multiple times that they would always be there for us if we had fallen away from the Church and wanted to come back. I needed to have my sins forgiven, and there was a deeply-rooted belief within me that this was the way to get it done.

On the way there, I remember thinking that afterward I would either go out drinking or go to an A.A. meeting. I did not myself know which. If I was right that sin, not alcohol, was my real problem, maybe I could get my sins forgiven and then be able to become a moderate, normal drinker. I guess that I was looking at confession as operating as a kind of exorcism. I don't think I thought this on a literal level, but I somehow expected that, if I could get back into a state of grace, my drinking demons would leave me.

I rang the doorbell and an old priest in a wheelchair came to the door. I recognized him from my high school days, although I had never taken a class from him. I told him what I wanted, and he wheeled outside. I don't know if I said that I wanted my confession to be a Fifth Step; I probably didn't say that. I told him that I

---

1. *Alcoholics Anonymous*, 59.

had been in A.A. and had not been to confession in many years. I wanted to tell him my story.

The priest did not want me to tell him my story. He said to me two or three times that he used to be a chaplain in the Navy and that he had already heard everything he needed to hear. He rattled off a short list of common sins, and he asked me if I had ever committed any of them. There were a couple of things that I had done and a couple of things that I had not done. He then asked me to mention one or two sins for which I was especially sorry. He told me to say the Act of Contrition as he gave me absolution and made the sign of the cross. He smiled and wished me well.

As I drove away, I was deeply disappointed. I had wanted something much, much more. I felt good on some level because I did believe that my sins were forgiven. My feelings, however, were mixed to say the least.

I can look back today and have some sympathy for that priest. Step Five and the Sacrament of Reconciliation may have some important points of overlap, but they are not the same thing. On the one hand, it is possible in an A.A. context for a priest to work through a Fifth Step with an alcoholic and make it double as a confession. On the other hand, it is not to be expected that an alcoholic can suddenly corner a priest and have him turn a confession into a Fifth Step. And perhaps that priest had other things he needed to do that evening.

At that moment, I was interpreting my experience through the lens of my own deep needs rather than trying to understand things in the big picture. In an earlier reflection, I described how in college I would decide not to buy any beer on a given day and then watch my car drive me to the beer store. This time I watched my car drive me to an A.A. meeting.

And so it was that I returned to the Catholic Church and to A.A. on the same night. From the way things happened, I came to believe that God wanted me in both organizations. They've been working together in my life ever since.

REFLECTION 17

Why I Needed A.A.

As I drove straight to an A.A. meeting after my disappointing confession, I'm not sure what I was thinking. I was too far inside the situation to be able to analyze anything. It was something like an instinct that brought me back to A.A. To the extent that I had hoped that a good confession would release me from sin and restore my agency so that I could gain control over my drinking, my hope had not been fulfilled. The priest, who to me represented the Catholic Church and stood in the place of God, did not want to hear my story.

In retrospect, I had a deep need to be able to tell another person as well as God the actual things that I had done. I was upset, and on some level I knew that a bar would be the last place I should go. I needed to go somewhere where I could talk with other people about the things that were bothering me. As I entered the room, I at first felt deeply ashamed for having gone back to drinking. That shame, however, was cast out as I encountered not finger wagging but rather smiles of relief that I had come home. "You're in the right place," is what they told me. It didn't take many meetings for my denial to start fading away. How was it that I could ever have fallen back into denial after writing a Fourth Step that detailed a long and obvious pattern of alcoholic behavior, often with tough consequences? It's crazy how the desire to drink can continue to influence you even after you had stopped drinking for a while.

I needed to get quickly and seriously down to work on my A.A. program. I reconnected with my sponsor and would eventually take my Fifth Step with him.

I needed A.A. because it was designed to address my disease of alcoholism in a way that the Catholic Church was simply not equipped to do. I was finally coming to a better grasp of the relationship between alcoholism and underlying problems. Yes, every alcoholic has underlying problems that need to be addressed. The thing is, if you are an alcoholic, you can't effectively tackle your issues without first achieving some continuous sobriety. If you don't stop drinking, no other progress is going to be made. In this sense, it is drinking that is the problem. The alcoholic must deal with their drinking first and foremost.

What happens over time is that, as an alcoholic stays sober, their underlying issues will arise, some of which may take years to surface. If these concerns are not addressed, it is likely that the alcoholic will drink again. Another possibility is that a person may stay away from drinking but cease to grow spiritually. In A.A., such a person is said to be "dry" but not "sober." In most cases, working through the Twelve Steps will be the most efficient way of tackling these matters. Many alcoholics find that they also need to seek help from psychologists, doctors, and other professionals.

That fall, I had a big challenge coming up. I was still taking courses to earn my teaching certificate. One course would require me to stand up in front of a classroom and teach my peers as if I were teaching high school students. Not only that, but the professor was also going to film the session so that he could play it back to the whole class while critiquing my performance!

Although I didn't know what to call my fear at the time, I had an anxiety disorder. I was deathly afraid to speak in front of any size gathering. When I knew I had a practice teaching session coming up, I would be terrified for a few days in advance, feeling as though my stomach was tied up in knots.

I talked about my fear of teaching in A.A. meetings that fall. By this time, I knew many of the people in the meetings I attended. I did get nervous, sometimes very nervous, before it was my turn to speak in a meeting. I was also, however, starting to feel more comfortable, and I often said things that made people laugh. One time I spoke about how when I first joined the program, I felt as though my real life was over. Now that I was getting sober, though, the move from being a drunk to becoming a recovering alcoholic felt more like a promotion.

Fear is a frequent topic in A.A. meetings, and recovering alcoholics know a lot of strategies for overcoming it without drinking. Sometimes alcoholics will say things like, "Up to now you got your balls out of a bottle. Now you have to learn how to face your fears without that crutch." Some people suggested prayer because you can trust in your higher power to give you courage.

The most helpful advice came from someone who asked me to think about the worst thing that might happen as I did my practice teaching. I said that I might forget everything that I wanted to say. "Is that it?" he questioned. "Is that really the worst thing that could happen?" I said that I might pee my pants. Everyone, including myself, started laughing, except the questioner, who continued: "Well, let's think about what would happen after that. What would happen after you forget everything you were going to say or if you pee your pants? Would you be able to survive those things? What would happen next?" I replied that I guess I would take a shower, put on clean clothes, and come back here and talk about it. I don't think anyone wet themselves, but we all continued to laugh pretty hard..

I was still nervous when I did my teaching sessions, but I knew it was something that I could survive. As this underlying issue surfaced, I was learning how to deal with it without using alcohol as a crutch. As a teacher and public speaker, I've had to confront this issue throughout my life. Over the course of many years, it became less and less of a problem. I almost never feel nervous in the classroom anymore, though I still can get anxious before I give a lecture in front of a large crowd. Yet almost always, within a few minutes, I start to enjoy myself.

A.A. not only helped me to stop drinking and to confront my fear of teaching, but also to address many other personal challenges.

WHY I NEEDED A.A.

As an alcoholic, I needed A.A.. There may be other places where underlying issues can be addressed, but for the alcoholic, no real progress is ever going to be made apart from confronting first the overlying problem—the drinking.

REFLECTION 18

A Shaky Re-Entry into the Catholic Church's Atmosphere

MY REEMBRACE OF MY Catholic faith moved gradually from an awkward uncertainty to an even more awkward certainty.

In my opening reflection, I compared my rediscovery of the treasures of the Catholic tradition to the ending of the film *National Treasure*, when many rooms lit up one right after the other. That image carries a lot of weight for me. The analogy really only works, though, if you can think of it being like time-lapsed photography. My A.A. experience lit the spark that would bring me back first to God, then to Christianity, and finally to being a practicing Catholic, in that order. That was indeed a lot of light to flood into my life in the space of less than a year. It would take many years, however, and much study, for that light to penetrate a multitude of rooms of my faith tradition and reveal the treasures that they held.

It was the disappointment I felt over my return to confession that drove me back to A.A. My return to the Eucharist, or Holy Communion, was also initially a mixed experience. The church building at my childhood parish was huge, even somewhat cavernous. The place made me feel uncomfortable. As I proceeded up the aisle to communion, I worried that many people would recognize me and might wonder what I was doing there. I had this weirdly paranoid feeling that my fellow Catholics would have a sense that I was doing something silly. My feeling of strangeness was irrational. After all, almost everyone there was receiving communion themselves. I was projecting my own doubts onto the congregation. So, even though I came to believe in God, read the gospels, and wanted to follow Christ, I was still experiencing some cognitive dissonance when it came to Holy Communion.

I don't remember how or exactly when this feeling of strangeness left me. It wasn't long, though, before I began to embrace the Catholic faith entirely and passionately. Catholicism had to be either the whole truth or nothing at all of the truth. I lacked maturity in my religious development. I relied a lot on my memory of my grade school catechism, much of which I had, in fact, memorized. My high school religion courses reflected the confusion of the transitional period that followed the Second Vatican Council (1962–65). For the first three years, these classes were mainly about psychology and personal meaning. My first-year high school religion teacher was a priest who spent many weeks talking with us about the film, "Alfie," which was about a man who used people and who basically led a meaningless life. At the end of that school year, that teacher left the priesthood and married a former Rockette from New York City, or so the rumor went.

My senior year religion teacher was a very conservative priest who tried to force us to accept hard to digest teachings about sex, marriage, and birth control. I stopped listening to him about two weeks after I became convinced that he had no interest whatsoever in listening to me or any of the other students. People who already know the truth sometimes have a hard time listening to the viewpoints of others. That person's last name is the current answer to my computer security question that asks the name of my least favorite teacher in high school.

In the early days of my recovery, I began to consume not only A.A. literature but also Catholic literature, much of which was highly conservative. I read Catholic fiction as well as defenses of the faith written by early 20th century British Catholics like G.K. Chesterton (1874–1936) and Hilaire Belloc (1870–1953), both of whom were sharply critical of the Protestant and secular milieu of England. I also read Thomas Merton's (1915–1968) *The Seven Storey Mountain*, his 1948 autobiographical book about how he became a monk. Although he would go on to become a leading progressive Catholic intellectual, much of the content of his first book was very traditional. It didn't take long for me to turn into a rather staunchly traditional and somewhat defensive Catholic. I became a bit like the priest who already knew the truth.

My religious conservatism became a source of friction between my girlfriend and me. Looking back, it must have been tough for a girl with healthy appetites in the years of the sexual revolution to have a boyfriend who was determined to live strictly by the Ten Commandments. I was myself not always perfect at keeping the rules, but still at times I spoke very judgmentally to her. We broke up over the combination of my inconsistencies and judgmentalism more than once.

With about thirty days of sobriety, I decided that smoking cigarettes, to which I had been addicted since my first year in high school, was a sin. Although I had heard general advice not to quit too many things at once, I enrolled in a ten-week behavioral modification seminar designed to purge my habit. Quitting smoking does not require anything like the total change in one's personhood that an alcoholic must accommodate to stop drinking, but the physical dimension of the addiction is more powerful. Recovering from alcoholism is the most important thing I have ever done and has required the most significant life changes. Smoking, however, is the hardest habit I have ever extinguished. I was able to quit in the early days of my recovery because it was a time of great transition in which all of the pieces of my life were being remade and rearranged. I have been free of cigarettes since December 5, 1975, when I was about one hundred days sober.

I finally took the Fifth Step formally with my sponsor, who was a good and simple man. I don't remember much about it. I don't think it was as emotionally dramatic for me as it is for many. But I did get to say out loud to God and to another human being the things that I had done.

A SHAKY RE-ENTRY

For the Sixth and Seventh steps, I made a list of my character defects and then humbly asked God to remove them. My main character defects were intellectual pride and spiritual pride. Intellectual pride is not just thinking that you are smart but thinking that being smart makes you better than other people. Spiritual pride is something similar. I can look back on my self-assessment now and still think that my judgment had been pretty accurate. Over the years, I have developed a stock joke on this subject, which goes: Through my spiritual experience, I received the deep and critically important insight that I am not better than anyone else. That insight was soon followed, however, by the realization that being one of the few people who truly understands that he is not better than anyone else makes me just slightly better than most other people.

For some tasks I might have been a bit too much for my sponsor to handle. I continued to work with him but also worked Step Eight and Step Nine with a religious brother who was a counselor at the college from which I had graduated. These steps require making a list of people we had harmed and making amends whenever possible.

In reaction to my having become very loose with the truth when I had been drinking, I now swung to the opposite extreme. I became scrupulous. I remember talking about stealing a piece of paper from a teacher's desk in fifth grade and worrying about how I was going to pay back the two cents. Should I put two cents in the poor box? I was still a sick person. My scrupulosity migrated to other miniscule matters. The brother finally said to me in a firm voice, "You have to put up a stop sign!" If I could make a list of the most important things that have ever been said to me, that line would be on it. That phrase has come into my mind at needed moments many times since then and has been a great help.

I think in retrospect that I was in a period of my life when I needed some basic things to be sharp and definite. You don't join A.A. with the intention of just cutting back a bit on your drinking. You don't just dip casually into the A.A. program here and there when you feel like it. You learn that you don't pick up a drink, not at all, one day at a time. The "How It Works" reading from the Big Book says, "Those who do not recover are those who cannot or will not completely give themselves to this simple program...."[1] It goes on to say, "Half measures availed us nothing."[2] I gave myself over completely to the A.A. program and to the God of my understanding. After a brief period of uncertainty, I reembraced my Catholicism with the same whole-hearted resolve.

---

1. *Alcoholics Anonymous*, 58.
2. *Alcoholics Anonymous*, 59.

REFLECTION 19

Balancing Factors

Although I did become quite strict in the practice of my faith, there were many things that helped me to keep life bearable for myself and for those around me. Both A.A. and the Catholic Church offered remedies for fanaticism and extremism.

My involvement in A.A. helped me to keep things in perspective. For all its stress on the need for total commitment and daily abstinence, A.A. stresses moderation in other matters. "Easy Does It," is one of the many slogans. High value is placed upon tolerance. There is a recognition that drinking can be a fine thing for the nonalcoholic who can handle and enjoy it. When it comes to matters of sexual behavior, the Big Book stresses not taking extreme positions.

A.A.'s openness to people of all faiths as well as to those of no faith helped me to balance my religious views. On the one hand, once my surface was scratched, the God of my understanding turned out at first to be the Catholic God of my youth. The catechism that I memorized in grade school taught that the Catholic Church was the one true church and was necessary for salvation. The only exception was for people who were invincibly ignorant, meaning that through no fault of their own they did not know that the Catholic Church was the one true church. On the other hand, however, it was apparent to my own eyes that God's grace was operative in many other places, especially in A.A., where on a regular basis people's lives were completely turned around for the better.

Alcohol Was My God—Part Four

I had heard some religious people in A.A. say, "A.A. saved my ass. My religion saves my soul." In other words, these people were making a sharp distinction that limits A.A. to treating their alcoholism and leaves matters of salvation to their religion. I agree that there is an important distinction to be made, but I could not accept the way that their phrasing downplayed A.A.'s spiritual dimensions. It seemed obvious to me that A.A. was saving a lot more than just people's asses.

This interplay between the importance of the ultimate truth of my faith and the conviction that God was evidently hard at work in many other places would accompany me in one form or another throughout my life. Although it began as a difficult and painful tension, overall, I believe it has been a healthy one.

My own interpretation of the gospels had already led me to appreciate the importance of recognizing the existence of points to be held in tension. There are certain things about which we will not comprehend the complete truth until the last day. Through my own personal experience of religious transformation, I came to believe that you can be in touch with the ultimate meaning of life without being able to completely explain it, even to yourself. Just because we can rightfully claim to have God's revelation does not mean that we fully grasp everything or even most things. My commitment to the truth of my religious tradition stood in healthy tension, not contradiction, with my acknowledgement that God remains mysterious and beyond our complete comprehension.

Reading the Lord's Prayer within the context of the Sermon on the Mount also helped to temper some of my tendencies toward extremism. The prayer asks God to forgive us our trespasses or sins as we forgive those of others. Along with the directive not to judge others unless you want to be judged yourself, I saw the teaching as a formula. You will be forgiven only to the extent that you forgive others. Throughout my life since then, I have maybe been too quick to forgive, too reluctant to hold people accountable—and for selfish reasons! There are many things for which I hope to be forgiven.

Unfortunately, in the early years of my sobriety, I could become judgmental and self-righteous toward people who were close to me. I thank God that I was able to identify my main character defects as intellectual pride and spiritual pride. Asking God to remove these and continuing to name and work against these traits helped me to smooth out a bit some of my pointed edges.

I have said that the God of my understanding turned out to be the Catholic God of my youth, but I should qualify that statement. My relation to the God of my youth involved a mixture of love and fear, with the balance leaning toward fear. Now the balance was leaning more in the direction of love. My experience in the rehab was of a God who loves and who can smile. And this God, who was still a God of justice, was even more so a God of mercy who loves everybody.

There were also elements of my early religious formation that helped me to moderate my path back into the Catholic Church. It had been emphasized throughout my education that Catholics are intellectual and open-minded, and so, thankfully, a kind of open-mindedness was also part of the mix. A sister in my grade school taught us proudly that Catholics accept science and do not have a problem reconciling God's creation with evolution. As with everything else in my somewhat literary mind, there was room for some ambiguity and even some paradox and mystery. There's something painfully enjoyable about becoming dogmatic concerning the need for open-mindedness.

Many things said in A.A. meetings got me thinking. Once someone spoke about how a psychologist told him that he was depressed. Then he came into A.A. and found out that he was only down in the dumps. I found that remark not only to be very funny but also worth pondering. In some cases, a person is clinically depressed and needs professional help and perhaps medication. In other cases, it might be a lot easier to overcome being down in the dumps than to overcome depression.

There is a general bias among recovering alcoholics against medications. Some degree of skepticism can be healthy insofar as drugs can be especially dangerous for alcoholics. Some drugs are overprescribed or prescribed improperly. There are cases in which the use of drugs can represent simply trading in one addiction for another. Not all physicians are up-to-date on alcoholism and its implications.

Some A.A. members, however, take this bias too far by advising other members to throw away all pills. Such counsel can be as dangerous as a lack of any caution whatsoever. Hastily tossing away anti-depressants can come at the risk of suicide. An official A.A. pamphlet, "The A.A. Member—Medications and Other Drugs," allows the use of medications to address serious conditions and offers a list of suggestions to guard against their misuse.

A review of some scant journal notes that I wrote in those early years tells me I sometimes felt depressed and lonely. Getting sober involves a long-term struggle. It's not always easy to go without drinking when you have been drinking for so many years. And even though you quickly make a lot of friends in A.A., it still takes a long time to establish deep and healthy relationships.

Despite my difficulties and struggles, I returned to the practice of my Catholic faith carrying with me an experience of feeling loved by my higher power, a glorious sense that life has ultimate meaning, and a commitment to following the commandments, especially the two greatest ones of loving God and neighbor. I had a sense that God could heal me from my illnesses and save me from my sins. I had personal experience of the importance of community support. These were the lights that would help me over the course of many years to be able to see into the bountiful treasure rooms of my Catholic tradition.

In my seventeenth year of sobriety, I read a novel by Anne Tyler (b. 1941), *Saint Maybe*, in which a young man unintentionally does something tragically wrong that results in the death of his brother. In reaction, he becomes the founder of his own extremely strict church. Over the years, however, he gradually gains perspective and opens up quite a bit. Although I never founded my own church, I deeply identified with that character. A.A. and the Catholic Church worked together to help me hold in tension the strict discipline that I needed with the openness and tolerance that I required just as much.

REFLECTION 20

Why I Needed the Catholic Church

Over time, I came to realize that, just as I personally needed A.A. because the Catholic Church was not enough to address my specific problem, so I personally needed the Catholic Church because A.A. was not enough to address the full meaning of my life.

During the first year of my sobriety, there was a member of my A.A. group who often repeated the line, "A.A. isn't enough." He said it many times at many different meetings. I don't think I've ever heard anyone else say that. Now, I'm still not sure what all he meant by it. The line stuck with me, though. The most basic meaning that I took from it is that it's important to have a life beyond A.A.. It's not good to have all your friends be fellow A.A. members. It's good to have a family. It's good to pursue an education. It's good to maintain interests beyond the issue of recovery. The line can also carry the meaning that many if not most alcoholics will benefit from some kind of professional help. It can also mean that many alcoholics will benefit from professing a religion.

Members at meetings also use the phrase, "the firing line of life." There is a strong sense that there is a life out there beyond A.A., and that A.A. helps alcoholics to live that life. The purpose of A.A. is more than learning how to participate in A.A. meetings. A.A. operates as a safe haven from the world where recovery can take place, but it is meant to be more of a launching pad than a lifelong hideout.

I do think there are legitimate exceptions to this principle, and I don't mean to judge anyone whose life circumstances have made A.A. become just about the only community of significance to which they belong. I know and respect many such people, and I think that A.A. is much stronger than it would otherwise be without them. I hold in dynamic tension the truth that a life outside A.A. is important with the complementary truth that those whose entire lives are centered around A.A. play an important role in the fellowship.

I was drawn back to the Catholic Church at first because I wanted to go to confession. Up until my promise to God that I would receive the sacrament, my strong desire was mostly or perhaps even entirely unconscious. In retrospect, I can see that my longing was just the tip of the iceberg. Underlying that wish was my need to return to the Catholic Church with all of its sacraments and other treasures.

A.A. is a program designed to help alcoholics to achieve recovery from alcoholism. Its spiritual principles, especially as expressed in the Twelve Steps, have proved useful not only to alcoholics and other addicts, but also to many human beings with everyday problems and weaknesses. Still, its core message is addressed to alcoholics. It is expressly not a religion and is designed to work in conjunction with all religions and worldviews. Bill Wilson did not found a Universal Church of Twelve Step Spirituality.

Christianity, especially in its Catholic manifestation, has a mission to express universal truth to be communicated to all human beings. I know that Christianity is not the only religion in the world, and I am well aware of and respect other religions and their members. I experience it as a healthy tension that my faith claims to be universal and yet God is present and active throughout the world as well as the whole universe in ways that are not limited by Catholic Church teachings and regulations.

Over time, I could see that A.A. was for alcoholics and that the Catholic Church had a message intended for everyone. A.A. brought people into a relationship with their higher power in a way that facilitated a spiritual awakening. The Catholic Church proclaimed a narrative about an all-good, almighty, and all-loving God who created the heavens and the earth. It offered a vision that included incarnation and resurrection, sin and forgiveness, redemption and sanctification, and judgment and eternal salvation. It spoke of a universe that included grace and sacramentality. It told a story that so moved my mind, heart, and soul that I came to believe it to be true. It helped me to relate with a higher power who loves everyone.

A.A. gave me the tools to address my alcoholism. I still belong to a group and have a sponsor. It was because of A.A. that I came to believe in God and then read the gospels. A.A. lit the spark that got my spirituality restarted. But I needed the Catholic Church. "Sister Molly Monahan" is a pseudonym for a religious sister who in 2001 wrote her own book about Catholicism and the spirituality of A.A. I can say with Sister Molly: "While I acknowledge with the deepest gratitude the ways in which A.A. has helped me to grow spiritually, I must also acknowledge that the seeds of its spirituality fell on the rich soil of the ancient Christian tradition in which I was raised."[1] I gradually came to realize that I got my ideas about the God of my understanding from my Catholic upbringing. My faith in the all-good and all-powerful God came right out of my Catholic background. Catholicism was my religion. For me, spirituality and religion worked together in a seamless manner.

With four months sobriety, I began a semester of student teaching in English Literature in a Catholic high school. I was intrigued by some factors that seemed to me to represent things that were beyond coincidence. When I was a first-year student in high school, I received the highest grade among one thousand students in the standardized English exam given at the end of the second quarter, right before Christmas. I liked the English teacher very much and found him inspiring. He was one of the reasons why I would major in English in college and then in my first graduate program. For the entire third quarter that began shortly after New Year's Day, however, I did not read any of the English assignments and received a failing grade. I'm not sure what was going on

1. Monahan, *Seeds of Grace*, 178.

with me. I was fourteen years old. My inexplicable disengagement didn't have anything to do with alcohol. I made a comeback in the fourth quarter and got a passing grade for the year.

The Catholic high school where I did my student teaching was one district over from my own school. My mentor was the same English teacher I had as a student. He had changed schools. The material, which included *Great Expectations* and *Lord of the Flies*, was exactly the same literature that I had failed to read eight years earlier. I had a deep sense that God was giving me a chance to live my life over and re-do a few things.

That summer, with just under one year of sobriety, I backpacked with my girlfriend through Europe using Eurail passes and staying in youth hostels. When we were in Rome and visited the Sistine Chapel, I was deeply engaged by the giant fresco, *The Last Judgment*, by Michelangelo (1475–1564). I focused especially on the detail of a young, muscular man sitting on a rock with one hand slapped over his eye. He looked as if he was thinking, "Oh no! What have I done? I should have lived my life differently. Now I am being sent to hell." I would later learn that this detail is a self-portrait of Michelangelo.

I had been accustomed to docents who explain religious paintings by referring mainly to the painting's history, who commissioned it, what techniques the artist used, and how it reflects the characteristics of a certain period. With my newly spiritual eyes, however, I had a personal insight into this treasure of the Catholic tradition. I connected directly with the religious theme of the Last Judgment. All human beings, including me, are going to face a final judgment. I don't want to end up like the young man with his hand over his eye.

I went to confession the next day in St. Peter's Basilica. There was some apprehension in my overall experience of *The Last Judgment*, but it was a healthy fear. My deeper reaction was to think that life has meaning, that it matters how I live, and that a just and merciful God is in charge of the universe. Such thoughts motivated me to live an upright, productive life and continue to stay sober.

PART FIVE

From Rigidity
to Open-Minded Inquiry

REFLECTION 21

Defender of the Faith

I VISITED ONE OF my old college English professors in his office in the Spring semester of 1976, and he encouraged me to apply for a teaching assistantship in the English department at a state university in the Midwest which happened to be where he had earned his own Ph.D. I took his advice and spent the next two years teaching first-year college English courses and earning a master's degree.

I arrived in my new setting that fall with one year's sobriety under my belt. I started going to meetings in the local A.A. right away. There were only three meetings per week in the area. I stayed involved, but not nearly as involved as I had been previously. I still would experience an occasional desire to drink, but the actual compulsion to drink left me. Being a recovering alcoholic had become deeply ingrained within my identity. I would tell just about everyone except my professors that I was in A.A.. The university had a reputation for being a drinking campus, but I did not have a problem staying sober. Later, people would sometimes joke: "You spent two years in that environment and didn't have one drink? You must be the only person ever to have done that."

Near the campus, there was a Catholic center where I attended Mass on Sundays with a number of my fellow graduate students. About a quarter of the student body was Catholic. The university itself, however, had a mostly secular and somewhat Protestant flavor to it. Being in such an environment somehow made me become very conscious of and vocal about my Catholicism. I talked about religion a lot both inside and outside the classroom. I wrote many of my papers on topics that were related to Catholicism. When I had to write a paper about Ralph Waldo Emerson, I wrote about his attitude toward Catholics. When I was able to design an individual directed study, I made it a course on Catholic novels. When I had to choose a three-course minor, I took courses in the Philosophy department in ethics and in religion.

One of my graduate professors was a Catholic priest. Another was Jewish. The rest were divided between Protestants and secularists. The priest at one time confided in me that there was a bias against Catholicism among most of the English faculty. Another professor told me that some of his colleagues wondered aloud how I could be so bright and still be a practicing Catholic.

I lived in a graduate dormitory my first year, and I made friends with people who came from many backgrounds. Although I have strong tendencies toward introversion, I became very outgoing during this period. I was also extremely honest to the point of being blunt. People had a hard time getting mad at me, however, because I had a manner that was, as several people told me, "disarming." I did truly try to love people. I was still in an intense period of personal growth, and I say, with some trepidation, that some people regarded me as very spiritual, even though not everyone had a high opinion of spirituality. For my first few years of sobriety, I carried with me a sense of being close to God, though with some up and down mood swings.

Not far from my dormitory was a cafeteria where the graduate students ate most of their meals. That made for a lively community where everybody knew each other and often had friendly debates. There were Science majors, Social Science majors, Foreign Language majors, Journalism majors, medical students, and many of my fellow English majors. Just about everyone knew that I was a recovering alcoholic and a vocal Catholic. I seemed to get along well with everybody. It used to be that I was loud when I was drunk and bound up inside myself when I was not drunk. Now I was sober every day and reaching out to people. I never did any embarrassing things on the level of what I used to do regularly. I was a good and loving person, rather intense, but likable.

I was in many ways a person of extremes. The university cafeteria had an all-you-can-eat policy. My weight had seesawed throughout high school and college. Most of the time I was somewhat overweight. Sometimes I was in decent shape because I worked my supermarket job and loved to drink more than I loved to eat. By the end of my first academic year, however, having consumed three unlimited meals pe day, I gained a considerable number of pounds. Several people pointed out the increase to me in a nice way.

That summer, I went to the opposite extreme. I went back to my hometown and worked my supermarket job full time. I joined my mother's Weight Watchers group. She prepared most of my meals, and I lost fifty pounds in twelve weeks. I came in at two pounds under my goal weight. Near the end of the summer, I visited a good friend of mine from the state university in a city not far from my hometown. This woman would later turn out to be my wife. She complained to me that I was now too skinny. I had never heard anyone say that before.

I spent my free time that summer with my old girlfriend. As the school year and my departure approached, we were seriously talking about getting married, although we didn't set a date. We still had struggles around my strong commitment to the Ten Commandments along with my inability to keep all of them, especially when it came to certain forms of intimacy.

Back on campus, having a sort of fiancé back in my hometown gave me the freedom to be friends with many women for my first year and a half without having to worry about romance or sex. That was for me a liberating experience and a time of much growth.

Just before Halloween, my sort of fiancé called me. She was upset. She had had a conversation with a girlfriend who warned her that if I was such a serious Catholic, I wouldn't let her use birth control once we were married. I don't recall my full response. I told her that I did not have an absolutely fixed position on the subject, but that I would probably want to follow Catholic teaching. She made an ultimatum: either I would promise her that she could use whatever method of birth control she wanted, or it was all over between us. I did not give in to her ultimatum, and she declared our relationship to have reached its end.

I felt very down for a couple of days. She had been in my life for almost four years and had gone through a lot with me. And now we had broken up.

On Halloween evening, the main street of the town was closed off from traffic. Halloween is a big night on that campus. Most students dress up in elaborate and creative costumes as skeletons, witches, pirates, and Star Wars figures. Visitors come from all over for the event. There was always a lot of drinking and drunkenness.

I went out with some of my graduate student colleagues. As we walked along the crowded street, I experienced a deep sense of being liberated. I didn't have any hard feelings toward my now suddenly ex-fiancé, but I was thinking more about opportunities for new relationships in my life. Maybe it's not always such a good thing to marry your first real girlfriend. Maybe there are other fish in the sea. Maybe it was time to experiment a bit. Maybe it had something to do with the fact that I had lost fifty pounds.

I would have a few romantic relationships over the next few years, some weird, some wonderful. One in particular was very serious on my part but didn't work out at least partly because of the intensity of my religious commitments.

I taught six first-year English courses over six trimesters. Due to my extreme nervousness, I always took the unpopular 8:00 a.m. slot. As I would explain back then, the class would be over by the time I would wake up.

Twice I taught the remedial writing course for students who lacked sufficient skills. I based my own approach partly on principles from A.A.. First, the students had to admit to having a problem. Then they had to come to believe that if they worked hard in this course, they would be able to attain college level writing skills. I did fine teaching the other courses, but I excelled when it came to working with students who had extra problems.

Although it was a state university, as the self-appointed Defender of the Faith, I rebelliously began every class I taught with a prayer.

REFLECTION 22

Forging My Catholic Identity through Encounters with Evangelicals

THERE WAS A FUNDAMENTALIST preacher who would sometimes wander across the campus of my state university, hollering, "Buddhists are going to hell. Jews are going to hell. Hindus are going to hell. Muslims are going to hell." I only saw him a few times. Most people found him to be rather entertaining. A few people would get angry and try to debate him. Seeing him helped to reinforce my Catholic identity. Whatever I was, I knew that I wasn't that. From the Catholic literature I was reading, I got the sense that God's grace can become available to anyone at any time. That preacher seemed to me to have no sense of ambiguity, paradox, or mystery. He apparently knew the Bible inside and out, but it seemed to me that there were some basic ideas that he just didn't get.

One of my fellow teaching assistants was an evangelical who was very serious about the Bible and faith. He thought of me as a "born-again Catholic." One time, he persuaded me to say that I accept Jesus Christ as my personal savior. I added, however, that I probably didn't mean the same thing as he did by my declaration. He took the position that I was most likely saved even though I believed in extra, weird Catholic stuff. I went to one or two evangelical services with him but would not partake of their version of the Lord's Supper.

In my second year, I moved into an apartment with him and another evangelical student who was very quiet. My friend and I continued to talk and argue about religion. He would distinguish between evangelicals and fundamentalists such as the campus preacher by explaining that the evangelical notion of total inerrancy left more room for interpretation. For example, extreme fundamentalists believe literally that the world was created in six days, whereas most evangelicals would allow for the word "day" to refer symbolically to an eon. My friend once explained to me that the Bible must be inerrant because the Bible itself teaches that it is. I replied that that is like saying that the pope is infallible, and we know this to be true because the pope himself has declared this infallibly. I recall that conversation so well because my friend saw my point and conceded it to me without reservation.

One day, my friend and I were in the main office for teaching assistants. I brought up to him what I saw as the contradiction between his being friends with the other TA's while at the same time believing that most of them were going to hell. I suggested to him that if he were to be consistent in the practice of his faith, he would be preaching to them day and night in order to save their souls. He responded that this is a topic well known and often discussed among his fellow evangelicals. They call it one of the "hard things."

Another time, in the middle of our final trimester together, we sat across from each other in our small living room. I forget the topic or who said it first, but one of us declared sternly, "I *hate* your doctrines." The other replied, "I hate *your* doctrines." We never spoke to each other about religion after that, but we got along just fine. I don't think that we truly hated each other's doctrines; we just had serious disagreements that stemmed from our different backgrounds. And we certainly did not hate each other. He is a very serious and respectable person. Even though in some ways I defined myself over against him, overall, he had a good influence on me.

Alcohol Was My God—Part Five

About fifteen years ago, this friend got in touch with me to let me know that he had become a Catholic, though I'm pretty sure I had little to nothing to do with his shift. Evangelical Christianity has evolved as a conservative political force since our days in graduate school in the seventies, and at the same time some powerful segments of the U.S. Catholic Church have developed right-wing tendencies. A number of former Evangelicals have embraced Catholicism.

As firm as I was in my faith during my graduate study of English, I was also haunted by intellectual questions, especially questions about other Christian traditions and other faiths. I didn't think that non-Catholics were all going to hell, but I had my own version of the "hard things" problem. One Friday night, I came across an undergraduate girl on the steps of a building on the main street of the town crying with her face in her hands. She had been dumped by her boyfriend and was feeling deeply depressed. She said some pretty extreme things that indicated she was in despair and didn't know what she was going to do. I asked her about her religious background. She wasn't going to church at the moment, but she came from an independent evangelical church in her hometown. She believed in that church but was taking some time off. She was not interested in the Catholic Church.

I was faced with a dilemma. On the one hand, I thought that involvement in a faith community would be the best direction for her to go in. My own experience told me that a person in a desperate situation needed both God and a supportive community. On the other hand, I hesitated because I feared that advising someone to go to a church that is not Catholic would be a bad and maybe even sinful thing for me to do. I didn't necessarily think that it was bad for a person to belong to such a community, just that it was a personal problem for me as a Catholic to advise them to do so.

My solution was to tell her that I was Catholic, and that I believed in the Catholic Church, and that it was hard for me to advise someone to go to a different church, but under the circumstances, I thought she should find a church in the vicinity that was similar to her hometown church. She should get involved and hopefully find there a group of people her own age with whom she could talk things over. She was touched by my earnestness in explaining where I was coming from and that nevertheless I was my still trying to help her. That strategy of just trying honestly to get everything out in the open has since proved quite valuable to me in many situations. It was the quality that made some of my fellow graduate students call me "disarming."

Incidents such as my encounter with that young woman helped to propel me to the study of religion and theology. For the following year, I applied to the doctoral program in English at the state university I was attending as well as to a couple of programs in theology at Catholic universities.

A few weeks later, the director of the English program at my university called me into his office to say that I was accepted with full support, but with the stipulation that he would have a talk with me about my problem of being too dogmatic about things. The difficulty wasn't just about my religious positions but even more about my being very opinionated and impossible to persuade about anything. I said that I knew what he was talking about. He thought that I meant my comment dismissively. "Oh no," he told me. "This is serious. The entire committee insisted that I have this talk with you." He had been warned that I would not take him seriously and would vehemently argue against anything he said.

I explained to him that by saying that I knew what he was talking about, I was acknowledging and accepting what he said. I told him a brief version of my story, how I had joined A.A. and had a life-changing conversion experience. I explained that the intensity of my experience was such that I became very strict and dogmatic, but that I was aware of this and was working on it. That man was so relieved. Obviously, he had been dreading the conversation. He appeared to be deeply moved and impressed by my story. He now looked forward to my entry into the doctoral program.

I was accepted by all three programs to which I applied with full financial support. I was deeply haunted by personal questions concerning faith and theology. In one of my applications, I expressed my personal goals in this way: "To be a teacher and a writer, a philosopher and a theologian." By the next fall, I was off to study theology.

REFLECTION 23

At Home in a Challenging Catholic Learning Environment

I WOULD SPEND THREE years as a teaching assistant in religious studies at a Catholic university in a large east coast city. Although I had been accepted into the doctoral program, at first I just wanted a second master's degree. My goal was to be a religious educator/minister in a parish and to write textbooks. I did well in my studies and was strongly encouraged to pursue the doctorate. I earned my master's degree in two years, and I then earned my Ph.D. in four more years, three of which I spent living in a city in the Midwest, married, writing my dissertation. My areas of specialization were Catholic theology and catechesis (religious education).

When I first arrived at my new university in fall 1978, I expressed interest in entering a seminary. I was not encouraged to do so. Starting around 1968, a large exodus of Catholic priests from the priesthood had taken place. By 1978, there was a lot of interest in fostering the theological education of laypeople. More than one person told me that, since I had an assistantship to study and would be around many priests and seminarians anyway, it might be best for me to postpone any decision. Although all of these factors were in play, I also think in retrospect that I was not encouraged to enter a seminary because they were reluctant to accept a recovering alcoholic with only three years' sobriety. For all I know,

Alcohol Was My God—Part Five

it might have been against the rules entirely. I know a good number of priests are recovering alcoholics, but their problem was not recognized until after they were ordained.

There may also have been an issue with me being very intense and overly enthusiastic at the time. Near the end of my first academic year, I remarked to my department chairperson that the more I studied theology, the more my sense of mission seemed to fade away. He replied, "Good. The world has enough religious fanatics. We need more people who can think intelligently." That same person, though, would later advise me to be sure to include on my resume that I founded and ran the "Religious Issues Discussion Group" for undergraduates on campus. He recognized my initiative as evidence that I was serious in what I was about. Starting that group was the direct result of A.A.'s influence on me.

With my background in literature, I thought that I might bring a challenging perspective to my new school. I was soon disabused of this notion and instead was quickly blown away by the level of sophistication of the faculty and of my fellow students. Many of my teachers were priests, brothers, and sisters. All my teachers were PhDs who published regularly. A few of the faculty were world-renown theologians. After the Second Vatican Council (1962–65), Catholic theology had become a booming academic enterprise. Intellectually, I was like a babe in the woods.

In my first week of classes, I encountered one of the world-famous priest-theologians in the hallway outside the main office of my department. I had come across his name while doing research at my previous school and had read one of his many books. I have a very readable face, and I was obviously upset. He asked me what was the matter.

I told him that I had just come from a class in a course on the Trinity. My teacher was a priest, but I got the impression that he didn't really believe in God. The priest-author smiled warmly and spoke to me in a fatherly manner. He told me that I should reserve my judgment on the course. That priest, whom he knew, was probably trying to get us to question our own narrow concepts of God before moving on to higher perspectives. He also said that

I shouldn't worry too much. He made a distinction between personal faith and theology. It's important to realize that your mind can be challenged while you still keep your faith strong. I have carried that advice with me throughout my life.

It didn't take me long to settle in and start feeling more comfortable. I found my coursework to be fascinating. Almost all my teachers and fellow students were Catholic. It seemed as though the air in that place was Catholic. In every room, Christ looked down upon me from the crucifix. I could relax and stop being so vocal and defensive about my faith. Quite the contrary, I was exposed to many different theological schools of thought and was free to pursue my own questions. Early on, I felt encouraged when I learned that the German theologian Karl Rahner (1904–1984) held that faith and philosophical questioning are fully compatible.

In my first semester, I had five courses. I was required to produce a research bibliography for one course and to write a research paper for most of the other courses. My papers were very different from each other, but they all drew upon different swaths of my huge bibliography on the problem of religious language. The technical term for my research area was hermeneutics, also known as theory of interpretation.

Religious language can be a suitable topic for academic study for at least two reasons. First, there is a gap between the words, concepts, and basic presuppositions of, for example, Christians of the first century and Christians of today. What are the interpretative tools that can help theologians to bridge that gap?

Second, one can make a basic distinction between first-level religious language that expresses experience immediately and second-level theological language that is more theoretical and often arises in response to difficulties that need to be sorted out within first-level language. Making this distinction can help to clarify why many statements that at first appear to be contradictory are not necessarily so. Things expressed on a commonsense first-level and things expressed on a more theoretical, secondary level both need to be understood within their own frameworks.

One encounters a good deal of first-level language in A.A. meetings. First-level language expresses experience in stories, images, and sayings. There is also a significant amount of first-level language in the Bible. I explained a bit in a previous reflection how my A.A. experiences gave me a helpful perspective for reading the gospels. One can almost hear going on in the background of scripture a lively conversation taking place in spiritually vibrant communities of faith. Many points of tension are expressed in a way that is not yet intended to reflect a consistent theological framework.

I was not hearing a lot of first-level religious language in the Catholic Church at that time. Some other Christian traditions have been more oriented toward personal testimony and faith-sharing. I was told as a child that good Catholics live their faith outwardly but do not wear it on their sleeves. Part of the reason for this characteristic may lie in the Catholic bias for formation over transformation and for the healthy-souled over the sick-souled. I retained a longing, though, for a Catholic Church that would include more encouragement for members to share their stories about how they grow in faith.

REFLECTION 24

Discerning the Presence of the Holy Spirit

As a Catholic, I believed in God as the Father, the Son, and the Holy Spirit. The Holy Spirit is the presence of God among us. I thought that the personal transformation I was experiencing had something to do with the Holy Spirit. I detected the presence of the Holy Spirit in A.A., although such a concept is not part of the A.A. program. I believed that the Holy Spirit was alive and well within the Catholic Church. Yet I also knew that not everything in A.A., or in the Catholic Church, or in myself came from the Holy Spirit. Like the will of God, the presence of the Holy Spirit needs to be discerned.

In my first weekend at my new university, I went to check out a charismatic prayer group that met on campus. I had some minor experience with the Catholic Charismatic Renewal in the past through the cousin who brought me to my first A.A. meeting. Charismatics are all about the Holy Spirit. Like Pentecostals, they speak in tongues, prophesy, and lay on hands for healing.

The service was in a fairly large venue, something like a gym. I intended to get involved. The charismatics I knew were both very Catholic and very passionate about their faith. They hugged each other a lot, something that greatly attracted me.

During the service, a young woman in a front row down and across from me was witnessing about her recent attendance at a large charismatic conference. She said, "And I realized that Jesus was standing right beside me." I said to myself, "Uh oh. This person is nuts." Then she went on to say, "And Jesus was also standing on this side of me. And in front of me. And behind me." For a second, I thought about Alfred Lord Tennyson's (1809–1892) "The Charge of the Light Brigade," where the cannons were in front of them, on each side of them, and behind them. Then it happily dawned upon me that this young woman wasn't nuts at all, but she was using what I was soon to learn to call first-level religious language. She did not think literally that the historical person Jesus was standing beside her. It was rather that she was aware of the presence of Christ in the people around her. I liked that.

I was grooving along with the service as we all prayed and sang. I felt like I was in the midst of a heavenly choir. The middle-aged couple standing next to me flashed smiles of approval. Suddenly, the man inquired when I had been baptized in the Spirit. I asked him what it meant to be baptized in the Spirit. His face dropped. His wife's face dropped. They looked at me as if I were an inferior creature. I was no longer in the groove. The man explained to me that there was an office in the basement of the building where I could register for classes to prepare for Baptism in the Spirit.

Even though I thought at the time that the Holy Spirit was already playing a significant role in my life, I did go down to the basement after the service. I intended to visit the office, but first I saw a priest hearing confessions. I hadn't been to confession since the day after I saw Michelangelo's fresco, *The Last Judgment*, and so I got in line. Although it had been quite a while back, within the span of time since my last confession I had had an intimate relationship with my girlfriend. I was often told that you can tell a priest anything because he has heard it all. This particular priest, though, got upset with me. He had disgust in his voice as he gave me absolution and an easy penance. I was turned off by his righteous style.

After that, I had a chat with a young woman who asked me how I liked the service. She quoted the Bible like a fundamentalist. I told her that I didn't interpret the Bible literally in that way. We argued a bit. I left without signing up for the Baptism in the Spirit classes.

I reacted against what I took to be an overall atmosphere of spiritual pride and exclusivism in the group. It was not up to me to judge their souls, but I did not feel comfortable with them. The tendency to think of myself as superior to other people was one of my own personal character defects that my A.A. experience taught me to guard against.

Several decades later, I described my experience of that prayer meeting in an address that I gave to a large audience at a conference. At the meal that followed, a priest who participated in the Catholic Charismatic Renewal sat next to me. He was very polite and respectful, but he did not like what I had implied about charismatics. He basically said that people in the renewal were quite aware of the difficulties to which I referred and that they have been seriously trying to address these issues for years. At the same time, the movement is much, much more than these problems, and it should by no means be defined by them.

I apologized to him. I identified my own experience of the Catholic Church in general with what he said about the charismatics. The Catholic Church has serious problems. Among other things, we have our own issues regarding the role of women, the inclusion of LGBTQ+ Catholics, and the historical treatment of colonized and enslaved peoples.

Especially troubling for Catholics have been the sex-abuse scandals, including cover-ups by bishops. I am convinced that clergy who sexually abuse children suffer from an addiction that, while not identical to alcoholism, has some deep parallels. In the 1980's, abusive priests were being sent to rehabilitation programs quite similar to those for alcoholics. For a time, it was thought these priests could be cured. We know now that there is no "cure" either for sex abusers or alcoholics. What is possible in both cases is for some addicts to achieve long-term abstinence, which in some cases can last until the end of their lives.

This lack of absolute certainty is one reason many (though not all) in A.A. refer to ourselves as "recovering alcoholics" rather than as "recovered alcoholics." I am an alcoholic who, by the grace of God and the fellowship of A.A., has not picked up a drink for nearly fifty years. I take it one day at a time. I sincerely hope that I will never drink alcohol again for the rest of my life. But I cannot guarantee it. If I am right that sex-abuse has significant similarities with alcoholism, then the only practical solution is to treat it as virtually incurable. And the way to treat those who might still continue to cover-up sex-abuse in any way is to condemn such behavior and remove the obstructors of justice from office.

The Holy Spirit is present and active in the Catholic Church, but by no means in all Catholic places at every moment. Many Catholics are dealing with the current problems, and we need to be working on them more. The Catholic Church and Catholic tradition, however, are much, much greater than these problems and should not be completely defined by them.

When I consider the active presence of the Holy Spirit, the first place I think about is A.A. meetings. I experience A.A. overall as something that has come from God. I also know, though, that not everything in A.A. is perfect. For example, members sometimes speak ironically and ashamedly of the "thirteenth step," which refers to sex with other members and can involve those with time in the program taking advantage of newer members.

I also think that the Holy Spirit is present in the Catholic Charismatic Renewal in a special way. I have wondered if I might one day find a charismatic prayer group that is theologically moderate. I truly feel a pull of attraction to them. I like and admire several charismatic Catholics. The ones that I know personally are humble people. To me, however, what I experienced as the group tendency toward exclusive superiority suggests that not everything in the renewal comes directly from the Holy Spirit. To me, that tendency is a deal-breaker. That could very possibly be my loss.

So, in my first week at my new school, I attended a prayer meeting that seemed disconnected from theological reflection. I also attended a theology class that seemed disconnected from faith. I sensed the need for places that valued simultaneously both first-level religious language and second-level theological exploration.

REFLECTION 25

Are You Talking to Me?

My main purpose in these reflections follows the basic directive in A.A. that we share our experience, strength, and hope. I have a need to tell you what happened to me, and for you, whatever your background, to take away whatever is worth something to you. Whether you are healthy-souled or sick-souled, religious or nonreligious, commonsensical or scholarly, I hope you can find that in some way I am talking to you.

It is not my direct intention here to specifically promote either Christianity or the Catholic Church. But maybe I am kidding myself; perhaps there is more evangelization going on here than I originally intended. I am obviously praising both A.A. and the Catholic Church to some degree. Unlike what I would say in an A.A. meeting, I am giving witness not only to my recovery through A.A. but also to my spiritual growth through my Catholic faith. What I absolutely want to avoid is to preach to alcoholics in A.A. that they should join the Catholic Church.

I have described how my experiences in A.A. lit the spark that started the crankshaft of my Catholic engine. What I still need to explain is how that spark started a chain reaction that lit up room after room of the treasures of Catholic tradition. I am not able to follow a strict chronology of how that happened because my insights and discoveries did not succeed each other in a strict linear fashion. It's as though the various rooms had automatic dimmer switches and that the light from one room would brighten the light in another room which in turn would make the first room yet brighter.

Of course, not everything in the Catholic Church has ever been or is now all sweetness and light. This is no small matter.

Much light entered the Catholic Church during the time of the Second Vatican Council (1962–1965). The Catholic Church had been withdrawing, at times recoiling, from the emerging modern world. The modern world brought with it its own mixture of light and darkness. It was characterized by a turn away from medieval metaphysics toward science, historical consciousness, and human experience. It gave us an awareness of universal human rights as well as the reality of total warfare, including nuclear weapons. It gave us our current forms of democracy as well as various forms of authoritarianism.

The Catholic Church needed to meet the challenges of the modern world without losing its own identity and mission. In its sixteen documents, the Second Vatican Council affirmed human experience and historical consciousness while still faithfully proclaiming the gospel message. The Council called worshippers to more conscious and active participation in the liturgy and to deepen the connection between liturgy and life. It presented divine revelation as being grounded first of all in a personal friendship with Christ and taught that scripture and tradition are the main expressions of this relationship. It identified what it named "the universal call to holiness" as central to the mission of the church. The Council also stressed the need for the faithful to pay attention to the signs of the times, to engage the modern world in dialogue, and to forge a new synthesis between faith and science.

I saw the emphasis on the universal call to holiness as comparable to A.A.'s focus on the need for personal spiritual growth. In A.A., you either grow spiritually or you eventually get drunk. You learn to listen. You hear the message, and you implement it. You find that the entire A.A. program is addressed to you personally, not in a self-centered way, but rather in a way that makes you reach beyond yourself to others and to your higher power. You start to live your life on a spiritual basis, seeking first the will of God.

I also came eventually to understand that the entire Catholic tradition was addressed to me—not only to me—but to me. For some reason, it strikes me as funny to think here about Robert De Niro in the classic scene from the film, *Taxi Driver*, looking into a mirror, striking an intimidating pose, and saying, "Are you talking to me? Are you talking to me?" Yes, the Catholic tradition was talking to me. It was talking about God, the meaning of life, and the call to grow spiritually as a loving person. It was talking about love of God and love of neighbor. The call to spiritual growth applies not just to individuals but also to communities. Communities include families, neighborhoods, parishes, schools, clubs, businesses, cities, towns, states, countries, the world, the universe, and the kingdom of God.

There is a saying in A.A.: "If you want to keep what you've got, you've got to give it away." That saying expresses one of many reasons why I continue to be involved in A.A.. It also motivates my studies, my teaching, my writing, and my continued participation in the Catholic Church.

In the reflections that follow, I relate some key insights linking my A.A. experience with my Catholic faith during my doctoral studies in theology. Then I make some connections with Pope Francis' call for each Christian to be able to grasp and to share their own personal synthesis of their faith as they integrate their religious tradition with the developments and challenges of the modern world.

PART SIX

Personal Synthesis

REFLECTION 26

The God of My Understanding Who Remains Beyond my Comprehension

MY EXPERIENCE OF SPIRITUAL transformation in A.A., especially the giving of myself over to my higher power, helped me to grasp the meaning and importance of the theology of the German Jesuit theologian Karl Rahner (1904–1984).

I entered the academic study of religion and theology as a traditional Catholic who valued the truth as expressed in the catechism of my youth as a rock to cling to in the midst of many storms. At the same time, I had a kind of radical open-mindedness that came in large part from my experiences in A.A.

Before I joined A.A., I was deeply convinced that I needed alcohol to live. I had started to believe that there might be a God, but I had no personal connection with that God. I was adrift in life and had no hope. Yet, in my confusion, I thought that I knew more than anyone else. I regarded myself as the center of a universe in which alcohol was the most important element. My spiritual transformation allowed me to see that my views were false. My deepest convictions proved to be illusionary. I became consciously convinced early in my recovery that I should treat no worldview as absolute. I needed to remain open to the possibility that I could experience yet further transformations and that my newly acquired convictions could be overturned.

Still, my radical open-mindedness did not translate into an anything-goes skepticism regarding truth. I held my own open-mindedness in tension with, on the one hand, a basic trust in reason and science and, on the other hand, an experience of the importance of belief. I had come to believe that a power greater than myself could restore me to sanity. That belief, in tandem with giving myself over to that power, was an integral dimension of my being saved from the hell of my drinking. That power was the God of my understanding. Gradually, I found that my relationship with my higher power matched up well with and was deepened by teachings within my own religious tradition: that I can know that God exists, that God is all-powerful and all-good, that God loves me and everyone else, but that I still will never fully comprehend God.

In my graduate studies, I found in the theology of Karl Rahner an approach to God that spoke directly to my recovering alcoholic soul.[1] Rahner was trying to reach out to a post-World War II Europe in which secularists and atheists were rapidly growing in number. Their rejection of God and religion was linked with their experiences of atrocities such as the Holocaust and total warfare, including the actual use of atomic weapons, as well as the apparently inadequate responses of God and the churches. Rahner was trying to awaken Catholics from the ideological slumber that would allow them to ignore or even to participate in such atrocities. Part of Rahner's strategy was to talk about God in such a way as to appeal first not to explicit Christian tradition but to universal human experience.

Rahner distinguished between two levels of human experience. There is a transcendental level, which is prior to what is expressed in words and concepts, and a categorical level, which is the more conscious level that can be expressed in words and concepts.

On the transcendental level, human beings are oriented toward a mystery that is beyond themselves. This is a mystery that

---

1. Rahner, *Foundations*, 44–89.

draws them outside of the narrow confines of self toward a larger world of truth, goodness, and love. Human beings are often tempted to accept as truth whatever is convenient for maintaining their own comfort. Yet there is also within each human being, at least potentially, a drive to want to know the truth no matter what it is, even if it is going to hurt. Rahner identifies this drive as an orientation to the absolute mystery that is God. This drive is also evident when one chooses to act in a truly good way even if it is not immediately good for oneself. One can further detect this orientation to the transcendent when one person loves another person in a way that treats that individual not merely as an object in one's own self-centered universe but as truly another person in their own right with their own personhood, will, dignity, and destiny.

Rahner's theology connected with my own experience of spiritual transformation. In giving myself over to the God of my understanding, I was at the same time giving myself over to a God whom I knew to be far beyond my comprehension. To seek out this God faithfully is to become a person who is radically honest, who strives to be good, and who does their best to be a loving person. Rahner was talking about me, yet at the same time he was talking about all human beings.

The transcendental level of experience is not unconscious, but it happens on a level of consciousness that is so deep that it is prior to any expression in clear words and concepts. You can talk about the transcendental level, but once you start talking about it you are operating on what Rahner calls the categorical level, the level of language, concepts, and categories. We know that God is beyond our imagination, but we still as human beings operate with images and concepts in order to relate with God.

Rahner described a phenomenon that overlaps with the A.A. insistence that a person who does not believe in God can still give themselves over to a higher power. He spoke of "anonymous theists."[2] These are people who reject God on a categorical level

---

2. Rahner, "Christianity and Non-Christian Religions," 132. Rahner used the term "anonymous Christians" more frequently than "anonymous theists," but the latter phrase is more relevant here.

but who live their lives authentically seeking truth, goodness, and love. In other words, a person operating on the categorical level of clearly expressed ideas might say, "I do not believe in God"; on the transcendental level, however, that same person might affirm God through their honest and loving embrace of their orientation toward absolute mystery.

My experience of the God of my understanding has a categorical side. I have to have some understanding of God if I am to give myself over to God. God can't simply be absolute mystery, period. I have to be able to discern God's will, and I know well enough that God's will for me is connected with honesty, goodness, and love.

It is important to remember, though, that our images and concepts, while helpful, do not by any means completely capture God. Many famous mystics have attempted to put themselves in contact with God in an immediate way, that is, in a way that transcends any mediation through categorical images or concepts.

In contrast to the transcendental path of the mystics, most popular forms of Catholic prayer are thoroughly categorical, making use of images and concepts drawn from scripture and tradition. In the early years of my sobriety, I relearned to pray the rosary. I found this treasure of the Catholic tradition to be a deeply meditative form of prayer that allows me to contemplate the mysteries of the Christian faith through the eyes of Mary. In the front of my mind, I recite Our Fathers and Hail Marys, somewhat like a mantra. At the same time, in the back, deeper recesses of my mind, I meditate upon various stories from scripture and tradition. I mix in thoughts about my everyday life as well as my prayerful intentions for others.

The extensive use of images in prayer corresponds with the Catholic openness to the use of various forms of material art in architecture and in worship. The Catholic Church is united in this openness with Eastern Orthodox, Anglican, and other high church Christian traditions. Iconoclasts take an opposing position, observing ancient prohibitions against the religious use of graven images. Catholics stress the goodness of all of God's creation, including material objects, as well as the power of Christ's Incarnation to redeem all that exists. If God can take on a material body, then material bodies cannot be all bad.

The Catholic world is filled with awe-inspiring churches, such as the Cathedral of Notre Dame, for which not only all of France but the entire world came together to rebuild after a devastating fire. Churches, monasteries, and museums display priceless works of art. These treasures of the Catholic tradition tell the Christian story with breath-taking splendor and beauty.

I find particularly fascinating Medieval and Renaissance paintings of the Communion of Saints, ones that depict saints from various centuries surrounding Mary and her child, Jesus. There are many such paintings by a variety of artists. What most engages me is their religious meaning. By putting figures from different centuries into the same painting, these artists are not displaying some medieval lack of historical awareness. They are, rather, depicting a scene in a world beyond this world. These paintings represent how Christian community transcends space and time and blurs the line between life and death. They depict an eternal realm in which all are interrelated through the love of God.

In some of these artworks, there will be one figure who looks directly out at those viewing the painting, often with a hand gesture that invites them into the scene. This motif is known as the "sacred conversation," indicating an ongoing communication between those in this world and those in the next.

As the Catholic priest, novelist, and scholar Andrew Greeley (1928–2013) put it:

> Catholics live in an enchanted world, a world of statues and holy water, stained glass and votive candles, saints and religious medals, rosary beads and holy pictures. But these Catholic paraphernalia are mere hints of a deeper and more pervasive religious sensibility which inclines Catholics to see the Holy lurking in creation. As Catholics, we find our houses and our world haunted by a sense that the objects, events, and persons of daily life are revelations of grace. . . . This special Catholic imagination can appropriately be called sacramental. It sees created

reality as a "sacrament," that is, a revelation of the presence of God.[3]

This sacramental imagination is something I grew up with, eventually lost, and then regained as I reembraced my Catholic faith.

An analogy can be drawn between, on the one hand, the Catholic sacramental imagination's appreciation of the relationship between the spiritual and the material and, on the other hand, Rahner's distinction between the transcendental and categorical levels of human experience. Just as Catholics do not reject the material in favor of the spiritual, so they do not reject the categorical in favor of the transcendental. It is rather the case that they experience the transcendental as present within and mediated by the categorical.

Being able to distinguish between the transcendental and the categorical levels of the experience of God helped me to forge some links between A.A. and my Catholic faith. Rahner's theological language about God as the absolute mystery toward whom I am oriented offers a second-level theological complement to A.A.'s first-level language about giving my will and my life over to the God of my understanding. The God of my understanding is a power greater than myself. God transcends me. My spiritual transformation took place in the deepest part of my psyche, in a place that is beyond words. Seeking the will of God draws me outside of myself, orienting me toward a mystery that is far beyond my own psyche, a mystery that is infinitely and eternally true, good, and loving.

---

3. Andrew Greeley, *The Catholic Imagination*, 1–2.

REFLECTION 27

Spiritual Growth Is Central to Theology

My experience of spiritual growth in A.A. gave me insight into the importance of the concept of conversion in the theology of the Canadian Jesuit philosopher and theologian Bernard Lonergan (1904–1984).

Spiritual growth is central to the Twelve Steps. If you want to achieve a lasting sobriety, you need to learn to live your life on a spiritual basis. Everything in A.A. is directed toward helping you grow spiritually. Yet this focus leads to the opposite of selfishness. All of it is designed to help get you outside of yourself. As you follow the steps, you learn that you have to get out of the driver's seat. You have to turn your will and your life over to your higher power. You have to let go and let God. You learn to function as part of a community. You learn to be humble and to give service to others.

Thus, all of the tools of the A.A. program are secondary to the fostering of spiritual growth that will give the alcoholic the ability to get and stay sober. Whether it be the Big Book, the meetings, the Twelve Steps, the various sayings, sponsorship, or the telephone, none of these things exist for its own sake. All these elements of A.A. are intended to support sobriety, building community, and carrying the message to other alcoholics.

Alcohol Was My God—Part Six

One advantage A.A. has over other communities that promote spiritual growth is that it has a reliable measuring stick: is the person staying sober? Is the person acquiring the ability to not pick up a drink one day at a time? Drinking is a tell-tale sign that something has gone wrong. There is one significant qualification: it is not uncommon for a person to stay "dry" without truly working their program or growing spiritually. Oftentimes, a member who drinks and then comes back claims that they had a long period of being dry before they actually picked up a drink. Abstaining from alcohol is, therefore, not an infallible measuring stick, but it remains a powerful gauge, nonetheless.

Bernard Lonergan developed a measuring stick for the accuracy and vitality of Catholic theology, one that can be extended analogously to all Christian practice. He placed conversion at the center of theological thought.[1] "Conversion" here does not refer to joining a religion or switching denominations. Lonergan uses the term to refer to ongoing spiritual, moral, and intellectual growth. Such growth represents "conversion" insofar as it involves an about-face or change in direction when considered in relation to opposite tendencies. What conversion measures is authenticity. Measuring authenticity requires discernment. Is the theologian faithfully rendering the actual Chrisitan tradition? Is Christian practice truly reflecting the spirit of Christ? Understood in this way, conversion functions in Lonergan's approach to Catholic theology in a way similar to how sobriety and spiritual awakening function in A.A. By emphasizing conversion, Lonergan spoke directly to my recovering alcoholic heart.

Like other scholars, theologians need to be able to engage in research, interpret sources, draw upon the sciences and the social sciences, construct histories, and engage in philosophical inquiry and debate. Claims made in these academic disciplines need to be judged in accordance with the rules of science and human reason. At the same time, theologians are committed to their traditions, to what they accept as God's revelation, to coherent renderings of their faith, and to the health of communities that live out that faith.

---

1. Lonergan, *Method*, 223–230.

Claims connected with faith commitments should not contradict reason, but, insofar as they rely upon tradition and belief, they cannot be fully demonstrated by reason alone. How can their truth value be validated?

Lonergan held that theologians must support faith claims by appealing both to reason and to the authenticity of their religious, moral, and intellectual conversion. Also relevant is the level of conversion evident in the theologian's faith community. For a theologian is not just an individual, but also at the same time someone who grows spiritually within a community of other people who are also growing spiritually.

I must admit that an appeal to conversion is not nearly as clean and simple a criterion as whether or not a person is maintaining their sobriety. Still, it is a way of acknowledging that theologians have loyalties and obligations that go beyond those of scholars in other academic disciplines as well as a type of measurement that can hold them accountable.

Lonergan does not limit conversion to spiritual growth, although that is a big part of it. He identifies three types of conversion: religious, moral, and intellectual. The religiously converted person is one who has fallen in love with God. This is a person for whom God ranks first among their life priorities. To be religiously converted is generally analogous to what A.A. means by a person who has a spiritual awakening. The morally converted person is one who makes decisions based not on selfishness but rather on trying to do what is truly good. Moral conversion aligns with the Twelve Step direction to seek and do the will of God.

What Lonergan means by intellectual conversion is rather complicated. I will try to describe it in my own terms by using the distinction between first-level religious language and second-level theological language. First-level religious language consists in personal testimony, sayings, stories, practical advice, and commonsense know-how. Second-level theological language is more analytical and theoretical, the language of theologians. It often arises in attempts to sort out difficulties or problems that can arise in first-level language.

People who lack intellectual conversion are unable to grasp the relationship between first-level religious language and second-level level religious language. They tend to be biased toward one or the other. A person who operates only on the first-level of commonsense reasoning might be inclined to reject most theoretical thought as overly complicated nonsense. For example, my evangelical friend read passages in the Bible about the need to explicitly affirm Christ in order to be saved and concluded that most of his co-workers were hell-bound. He lacked a theological perspective that could help him to separate what is true in a particular statement from unfortunate implications that may not be true. A more thoughtful approach could allow him to understand such declarations as representing first-level religious language, with consequences that cannot be projected onto all human beings everywhere. On this point, he differed little from the fundamentalist preacher who crisscrossed the campus announcing the eternal damnation of all non-Christians.

Conversely, a person good at theory can tend to reject first-level religious language as simply untrue or even superstitious. My initial reaction to the young woman at the charismatic service who said that Jesus was standing right next to her reflected my lack of appreciation for her first-level means of religious expression.

The intellectually converted person can appreciate both first-level religious language and second-level theological language as well as the relationship between them. Such a person knows enough about the working of their mind to be able to sort out and explain the meaning of various forms of expression.

Lonergan thought that most people live simply in the realm of common sense. There are many who do achieve various types of theoretical thinking. He thought that few people attain intellectual conversion.

The world of Catholic theologians is not completely free from bias against first-level religious language. Theology, which operates on a theoretical level, should done in service to the everyday faith world of ordinary believers. It is sometimes the case, however, that theology is regarded as offering a superior worldview that gives its practitioners a privileged status. Whereas it is true that theology rightly seeks a higher viewpoint, it is not meant to produce an alternative, intellectually detached world. Fortunately, most theologians bypass this detour into elitism and instead maintain the relevance of theological work for the practice of faith.

In A.A. meetings, one encounters a good deal of first-level language. People give testimony, share their experience, recite sayings and slogans, give practical advice, and offer commonsense solutions to problems. If two members say things that seem to contradict each other, that's ok. Not everything has to be sorted out on some analytical level. Individual members are free to take what they need and leave the rest behind. There is an understandable tendency to downplay theoretical thought

In contrast, Catholics are known to value learning and intellectual vigor. On the one hand, the Catholic Church is a huge global organization in which can be found communities of mutual support where first-level language is used. On the other hand, in comparison with many other Christian traditions that stress personal witness and testimony, there is a smaller percentage of such communities. Catholics are not generally known for their faith-sharing abilities.

I do find in A.A. an intellectual humility that recognizes that there are areas of knowledge and specialization beyond A.A.'s competence. Such recognition, however, is often accompanied by humorous takedowns of those who are intellectually pretentious. I myself have often benefited from being the brunt of such sarcasm. For me, one of the most helpful A.A. gems of wisdom is KISS: Keep it simple, stupid. I also like the saying: if you're so smart, what are you doing here? These adages were uttered more often in the early years of my recovery; in our politically correct times, one rarely hears these sayings. Overall, though, one of the most useful lessons of A.A. to help combat my English-major grandiosities was learning to live by simple slogans that I would have distained as clichés before entering the A.A. program. Easy does it! First things first! One day at a time!

A.A. is exceptionally good at fostering the first two types of conversion—religious and moral. Lonergan's emphasis on the centrality of conversion helped me to link my A.A. experience with my Catholic faith by showing how good theology must grow out of good everyday living. For understandable reasons, the A.A. program shies away from theorizing and philosophizing, leaving that to others. The Catholic Church, however, cannot afford to dismiss philosophical and theological thought. The Catholic tradition spans at least two thousand years, and the whole range of human history and creation is relevant to it. There is a lot to be sorted out. A Catholic theologian needs to be religiously, morally, and intellectually converted in order to maintain the crucial ties between simple faith and rigorous academic thought.

REFLECTION 28

Three Meanings of "Synthesis"

MY A.A. EXPERIENCE OF learning to share my story has helped me to understand and appreciate what Pope Francis (b. 1936) means by synthesis and synodality as well as why these concepts are so important for the future of the Catholic Church.

Pope Francis encourages all Christians to be able to share their own personal synthesis of their faith. He explored this theme in depth in one of his earliest papal documents, his 2013 *Evangelii Gaudium*.[1] He used the Spanish word, *síntesis*, which is translated into English as "synthesis," with connotations that are different from its English cognate. In English, "synthesis" is relatively formal. It's something intellectual. It's something that scientists and other academics achieve. It can have this meaning in Spanish, but, as Francis uses the word, it's more connected with personal experience.

Some of Francis' comments about synthesis were made in a section directly addressed to priests about how to construct good homilies. I take the liberty, however, of applying the term to the call to evangelization that Francis addresses to all Catholics. Francis himself stresses that "we are all missionary disciples."[2]

First, for Francis, synthesis has to do with your personal grasp of your faith within your own heart. Second, it has to do

---

1. Pope Francis, *Evangelii Gaudium*, para. 129, 143, 210, 230.
2. Pope Francis, *Evangelii Gaudium*, para. 119–21.

with how you express and communicate what is most important to you. It's almost the opposite of giving an objective summary of Christian teachings and practices. Your synthesis involves understanding and communicating your experience of faith in the most personal of ways.

Pope Francis uses the word "synthesis" with a third meaning that goes beyond the first two. For this meaning, he draws upon a document of the Second Vatican Council, *Gaudium et Spes* (Pastoral Constitution on the Church in the Modern World).[3] This document called for Catholics not to reject the world in which they live, but to be in dialogue with it. It advocated "reading the signs of the times." It encouraged Catholics to become "artisans of a new humanity." Catholics are called to achieve a synthesis of their faith tradition with the developments of the modern world, many (though by no means all) of which are positive.

Francis' first two meanings of synthesis overlap with the program and practices of A.A. The Twelfth Step of A.A. states:

> Having had a spiritual awakening as the result of these Steps, we tried to carry this message to alcoholics, and to practice these principles in all our affairs.[4]

Recovering alcoholics in A.A. carry the message by sharing their stories. Having a personal story and sharing that story corresponds with Francis' first two meanings of synthesis. Francis wants Christians not simply to quote the Bible or read from out of a catechism. He encourages Christians to have an internal grasp of the meaning of their faith such that they can give witness using their own words in a way that comes from the heart. Francis is concerned that many Catholics do not have such a personal synthesis. In order to be able to share the message of the gospel, many Catholics need first to be themselves awakened to the message of the gospel.

In recent years, Francis has been enthusiastically promoting a process known as "synodality." The roots of this term lie in two Greek words which, when combined, mean "to journey together."

---

3. *Gaudium et Spes*, para. 43; 56; 61.
4. *Alcoholics Anonymous*, 60.

THREE MEANINGS OF "SYNTHESIS"

The concept of synthesis is deeply intertwined with the synodal process. Francis hopes that the entire People of God, clergy and laity alike, will share their faith with each other as they tackle together the challenges posed by the modern world. He wants bishops, the final decision-makers for the Catholic Church, to act in a broadly consultative manner. He urges bishops to truly listen to all Catholics, including those who are presently alienated from the Church, as well as to other Christians, and to those of other faiths and worldviews.

When Pope Francis calls for every Catholic to be able to share their story of faith as well as to journey together, in my own recovering alcoholic mind I hear him saying that the Catholic Church needs to become more like A.A. In A.A. can be found a significant number of members who relate with God on a personal level and who are able to share their story with others. Anyone in A.A. who has any considerable amount of sobriety acts as a full representative of A.A. The members are there to share their message with the alcoholic who still suffers.

In the Catholic Church, if someone reaches out for help with a difficulty with their faith, they are likely to be referred to a priest, sister, brother, or professional lay minister. It is the rare Catholic who is ready on the spot to share their own story of faith with a fellow human being who is struggling.

I have heard more than one ex-Catholic recovering alcoholic testify that, before coming into the program, they believed there is a God, but they did not know what that really meant for them. In A.A., that deficiency is corrected. They develop a personal relationship with their higher power, one that most recovering alcoholics refer to as God.

Many Catholics practice their faith just fine. Most are of the healthy-souled rather than the sick-souled variety. They have been well-formed and well-educated in their faith. They live the life of grace through the sacraments and in the midst of their daily activities. They are not necessarily in need of some dramatic transformation to move them out of the darkness into the light. They would not benefit from the intense levels of sharing that A.A.

justifiably encourages for those urgently in need of recovery. Such emotional stripping down would be unnecessarily invasive and inappropriate in most Catholic settings. For example, talking about horrible things that one did prior to sobriety in a regular church faith-sharing group would be more disruptive than helpful.

In the contemporary United States, however, many Catholics could benefit from an increased focus on knowing and sharing their faith. Whereas several decades ago there used to exist a thriving Catholic subculture, there is now a complex, pluralistic mix of backgrounds and worldviews. These worldviews are both formed and malformed within a social media-soaked environment. The culture is deeply polarized.

I don't want to offer an unrealistic, sentimental picture of the days gone by. I do think, though, that it is harder to be a practicing Catholic today than it had been a few decades ago when the Catholic subculture was so strong and pervasive as to allow Catholics to live in a Catholic world. They lived out an interconnection with God and others. They were not as much in need of being in touch with their own personal faith story. The story of their faith was built into their everyday world. In the absence of that subculture, many Catholics need to heighten their awareness of their interconnection with God and others.

Synodality is designed to address the lack of synthesis—in all three of its meanings—in the church today. The polarization that infects society also mars the Church. There are pressing issues that urgently need to be addressed if the Catholic Church is to remain vital in the United States, Europe, and many places throughout the world. The Church needs to stop bleeding members, especially among the youth. Catholic leaders themselves disagree sharply over how to tackle these problems.

There is a deep theological division between those who want to adapt more thoroughly to what they see as positive developments in contemporary culture and those who think that there have already been too many changes in the traditional teaching of the Church. The process of synodality puts Catholics of different ranks and opinions in conversation with each other so that they can pray together, share their stories, and deepen their unity in faith. In other words, synodality is based on the proposition that any progress to be made regarding the third meaning of synthesis—engaging what is good in the modern world— must build upon radical and dramatic improvements regarding the first two meanings of synthesis—being in touch with and sharing stories of faith. The lack of unity resulting from theological disagreements can only be healed by forging a deeper sense of unity experienced in intimate, authentic fellowship.

Francis' third meaning of synthesis has some points of overlap with the A.A. program. The Big Book offers advice about how recovering alcoholics can engage the world. The basic approach advocated is to be moderate and reasonable, to avoid extreme positions, and to have respect for religious traditions even if one does not belong to one oneself. A.A. prepares a person to operate on "the firing line of life." The very last phrase of the Twelfth Step is "to practice these principles in all our affairs."

Unlike the Catholic Church, however, A.A. does not offer a centuries-long religious tradition that needs to be brought into a synthesis with developments in the modern world. It does not offer a narrative about the ultimate meaning of life that includes specific teachings about creation, human history, judgment, and eternal life. It does not have sacraments, specific moral rules, or social teachings that address issues such as marriage, immigration, economic justice, peace, and ecology. A.A.'s message and membership are limited to those who suffer from alcoholism and other life-devastating addictions.

A.A. offers a spiritual program of recovery, but it is not a religion. It does an excellent job when it comes to Pope Francis' first two meanings of synthesis—having a personal grasp of your message and being able to share it. Catholicism (along with other forms of Christianity) is a religion that must also address the third meaning of synthesis. It carries forward a long tradition of teachings and practices that Catholics need to integrate with their experience of the many challenges of the modern world.

REFLECTION 29

More on the Third Meaning of "Synthesis"

MY CATHOLIC FAITH INFLUENCES my participation in A.A. meetings. Once many years ago, someone in an A.A. meeting brought up the problem of his impending divorce. For financial reasons, he and his wife and a couple of small children were still living in the same house. As is often true in A.A. meetings, he didn't offer a lot of details. He just spoke in general about how difficult his situation was.

We went around the room addressing the problem he had raised. Many recovering alcoholics have been divorced, sometimes more than once. Person after person spoke about their own divorce(s) in the hope of saying something helpful. Much of the conversation revolved around the point that, no matter how painful the experience was, he did not have to pick up a drink. Drinking was not going to help him. In fact, it would make things many times worse. Much was also said about making use of the tools of the program: going to meetings, reading the Big Book, working with a sponsor, working the steps, making phone calls, and finding ways to help other alcoholics.

When it came my turn to speak, I said things that sounded a lot different from the others. I didn't know whether the decision to divorce was more his idea or his wife's or both, but I said that if they were still living together, and since they had small children, they really should consider trying to work it out. I spoke of my own marital difficulties. I added things about counseling students whose parents had divorced and of how devastating that can be for them. I mentioned something both humorous and wise that my mother once said: "Dennis, if your father and I believed in divorce, we would have gotten divorced many, many times. But we didn't believe in it, and so we stuck it out, and we're both glad we did." I also acknowledged that the man's actual situation might be something that didn't fit within the framework of my remarks.

My comments were received just like anyone else's. There was no change in mood or general sense of awkwardness. Most of the people who spoke after me returned to sharing their experience about going through a divorce and how they handled it. After the meeting, I mentioned to a friend that I felt a bit uncomfortable because my own comments were so different from everyone else's. Maybe I should have been more accepting of the man's situation and more sensitive about potentially making him feel guilty about the impact on his children. My friend responded that he thought it was good that I said what I did. He said further that I had shared my experience, strength, and hope and that I am someone who lives the way he talks. The man had heard from a variety of people. It was up to him to judge whether or not my particular remarks applied to his life.

As a Catholic, I have a basic bias against divorce. My Catholic tradition teaches that marriage is a sacrament that is supposed to last as long as both partners live. Despite my bias, though, I am not completely opposed to all divorce. Some marriages are plagued by abuse, violence, addictions, abandonments, and betrayals. Even the Catholic Church requires that a civil divorce be obtained if a couple applies for an annulment declaring that a sacramental marriage never really existed. I live in a pluralistic world in which not everyone is Catholic. As a Catholic, I have to live out a personal synthesis between my traditional modes of thought and the complexities of life in modern society. It's a bit like trying to balance while riding a wave. There's a dynamic tension between, on the one side, my deeply held beliefs and values and, on the other side, the thorny intricacies of real life.

At that A.A. meeting, I do not think of myself as speaking officially as a Catholic imposing my religion on someone else, but rather as a human being who had been formed as a Catholic and who was sharing from his heart with another alcoholic. Still, my predisposition against divorce didn't come from A.A. It came from my Catholic tradition.

I want to say that my marriage is a good marriage, not a bad one. Like all married couples, though, my wife and I have lived through ups and downs and at times have had serious struggles. But, like my parents, we didn't believe in divorce, and so we worked it out, and we're glad we did. And so are our children.

I do want the Catholic Church to become a bit more like A.A. when it comes to the first two meanings of synthesis—knowing your story in your heart and being able to share it in your own words. A.A., however, is not my religion. It is the Catholic Church that provides me with my worldview, my creed, my sacraments, my sense of the mysterious meaning of life, and my concepts and images of God. Having a religion with a tradition that includes specific teachings calls for me to live out Pope Francis' third meaning of synthesis in engagement with the modern world.

REFLECTION 30

Alcohol Is No Longer My God

SHARING MY OWN PERSONAL synthesis of my faith is what I have intended to do throughout these reflections. I owe my faith ultimately to God, but it has been mediated to me through both A.A. and the Catholic Church.

I've learned a lot by writing these reflections. I understand better now how A.A. and the Catholic Church each furnish me with things that I greatly need, things that the other organization is not equipped to provide.

I came to the realization in the first year of my sobriety that not only had I been living in denial of my problem of alcoholism, but also that I had been living in denial of the Catholic faith in which I had been formed. That Catholic faith resurfaced for me once I started relating to God as my higher power. I have spent much of my sober life studying the Catholic Church and Catholic theology. I love the Catholic Church, warts and all. I have had many great experiences connected with Catholic parishes, schools, faith groups, and friendships. By the way, when I was three years sober, I called the person who had disinvited me to his wedding, and we have been friends ever since.

The Catholic Church faces many challenges today. Deeper, however, than any controversial issues threatening the well-being of the Church, as pressing and unavoidable as these matters are, are these basics: the Christian story, the sacraments, knowing right

Alcohol Was My God—Part Six

from wrong, the virtues, the lives of the saints, a vision of justice, the coming of the kingdom of God. My Catholic faith is a great gift that connects me with people not only in the present but also throughout history and into the future in a way that transcends the boundaries of heaven and earth. Before I came back to the Catholic Church, I had been living in a world of darkness, pain, and confusion.. Now, as a Catholic, I wake up every morning into a universe that has been created by a loving God with a purpose. Anyone who truly pays attention can discern that, despite our real sufferings, this universe is bursting with meaning, even if that meaning remains beyond our full comprehension.

It is the People of God who are the Church. Every Catholic to some degree represents the Catholic Church. We all must take on the difficulties and strive to make things right. Among other things, it is important to reach out and offer support to those who have suffered at the hands of the Church.

I've had a sober life for now approaching half a century. I have my ups and downs, and I'm far from being perfect. But I love being sober. I love knowing what I did last night. I love not having horrible hangovers that last for days. I love not feeling full of shame, guilt, confusion, and defensiveness. I love having long-term, deep relationships. I love that I've been able to spend my life as a son, sibling, husband, father, grandfather, teacher, friend, writer, speaker, and traveler. I have my faith.

My faith today is deeply rooted both in A.A. and in the Catholic Church. Each gives me a critical perspective on the other. Each helps me to affirm the other. A.A. is a place where I experienced a miracle. I showed up in despair, and A.A. gave me hope. A.A. taught me that if I turned to God, God could and would save me from my alcoholism, and that's what happened.

I've read a few things about A.A., but for the most part I don't study it. I just live it. I love A.A. It's a place where I listen and give witness.

Fifty years ago, A.A. taught me to relate to God as my higher power, to God as I understand God. Over time, I have gleaned what inklings I have of God, my basic concepts and images of God, from my Catholic faith. I believe that the higher power I encounter in A.A. is the same true God whom I worship through the Catholic Church.

Alcohol is no longer my God. Drinking is no longer of ultimate concern to me. Of inestimable importance to me are my family, my friends, my neighborhood, my church, my A.A. group, my university, and my life's work. What is even more important to me is my sobriety because, without that, I would have nothing else. What is of ultimate concern to me is to seek and do the will of God. That is not to say that I am all that great at it. But without having accepted a reorientation of my life toward my higher power, I would not have been given my sobriety, the gift through which God has made all other things possible.

Appendix 1

The Twelve Steps of Alcoholics Anonymous

1. We admitted we were powerless over alcohol—that our lives had become unmanageable.
2. Came to believe that a Power greater than ourselves could restore us to sanity.
3. Made a decision to turn our will and our lives over to the care of God as we understood Him.
4. Made a searching and fearless moral inventory of ourselves.
5. Admitted to God, to ourselves, and to another human being the exact nature of our wrongs.
6. Were entirely ready to have God remove all these defects of character.
7. Humbly asked Him to remove our shortcomings.
8. Made a list of all persons we had harmed, and became willing to make amends to them all.
9. Made direct amends to such people wherever possible, except when to do so would injure them or others.
10. Continued to take personal inventory and when we were wrong promptly admitted it.

THE TWELVE STEPS OF ALCOHOLICS ANONYMOUS

11. Sought through prayer and meditation to improve our conscious contact with God as we understood Him, praying only for knowledge of His will for us and the power to carry that out.

12. Having had a spiritual experience as the result of these steps, we tried to carry this message to alcoholics, and to practice these principles in all our affairs.

(Source: *Alcoholics Anonymous*, 4th edition, 59–60.)

Appendix 2

The Twelve Traditions of Alcoholics Anonymous (short form)

1. Our common welfare should come first; personal recovery depends upon A.A. unity.

2. For our group purpose there is but one ultimate authority—a loving God as He may express Himself in our group conscience. Our leaders are but trusted servants; they do not govern.

3. The only requirement for A.A. membership is a desire to stop drinking.

4. Each group should be autonomous except in matters affecting other groups or A.A. as a whole.

5. Each group has but one primary purpose — to carry its message to the alcoholic who still suffers.

6. An A.A. group ought never endorse, finance, or lend the A.A. name to any related facility or outside enterprise, lest problems of money, property, and prestige divert us from our primary purpose.

7. Every A.A. group ought to be fully self-supporting, declining outside contributions.

THE TWELVE TRADITIONS (SHORT FORM)

8. Alcoholics Anonymous should remain forever non-professional, but our service centers may employ special workers.
9. A.A., as such, ought never be organized; but we may create service boards or committees directly responsible to those they serve.
10. Alcoholics Anonymous has no opinion on outside issues; hence the A.A. name ought never be drawn into public controversy.
11. Our public relations policy is based on attraction rather than promotion; we need always maintain personal anonymity at the level of press, radio, and films.
12. Anonymity is the spiritual foundation of all our traditions, ever reminding us to place principles before personalities.

(Source: *Alcoholics Anonymous*, 4th edition, 562.)

Bibliography

Alcoholics Anonymous. *The Story of How Many Thousands of Men and Women Have Recovered from Alcoholism.* Known as the Big Book. 4th Edition. New York: Alcoholics Anonymous World Services, 2001.
"The A.A, Member—Medications and Other Drugs." New York: Alcoholics Anonymous World Services, 2018. https://www.aa.org/sites/default/files/literature/p-11_0324.pdf
"The A.A. Preamble." New York: A.A. Grapevine, 1947. https://www.aa.org/sites/default/files/literature/smf-92_en.pdf
Aquinas, Thomas. *Summa Theologiae.* [Latin original c. 1269–74, unfinished.] https://ccel.org/a/aquinas/summa/home.html
Augustine, Saint. *The Confessions.* Translated by Maria Boulding, O.S.B. Hyde Park, NY: New City Press, 1997 [Latin original 397–400 CE].
"The Bill W.–Carl Jung Letters," *The AA Grapevine*, Jan. 1963. https://www.silkworth.net/wp-content/uploads/2020/07/The-Bill-W-Carl-Jung-Letters-Jan-1963.pdf
DeMille, Cecil B., dir. *The Ten Commandments.* Motion Picture Associates, 1956.
Dickens, Charles. *Great Expectations.* London: Chapman and Hall, 1861.
Emerson, Ralph Waldo. "Nature." In *American Literature Survey: The American Romantics, 1800–1860.* Edited by Milton R. Stern and Seymour L. Gross, 229–67. New York: The Viking Press, 1968.
Francis, Pope. *Evangelii Gaudium.*2013. https://www.vatican.va/content/francesco/en/apost_exhortations/documents/papa-francesco_esortazione-ap_20131124_evangelii-gaudium.html
Gilbert, Lewis, dir. *Alfie.* Sheldrake Films, 1966.
Golding, William. *Lord of the Flies.* London: Faber & Faber, 1954.
Greeley, Andrew. *The Catholic Imagination.* Berkeley: University of California Press, 2000.
Griffin, Kevin. *One Breath at a Time: Buddhism and the Twelve Steps.* Emmaus, PA: Rodale, 2004.
Hardy, Thomas. *The Mayor of Casterbridge: The Life and Death of a Man of Character.* London: Smith, Elder & Co., 1886.
Haughton, Rosemary. *The Transformation of Man.* Springfield, IL: Templegate, 1967.

BIBLIOGRAPHY

James, William. *The Varieties of Religious Experience: A Study of Human Nature.* New York: The Modern Library, 2002.

Landis, John, dir. *National Lampoon's Animal House.* Universal Pictures, 1978.

Lonergan, Bernard. *Method in Theology.* Edited by Robert M. Doran and John D. Dadosky. Collected Works of Bernard Lonergan, Volume 14. Toronto: University of Toronto Press, 2017 [original 1972].

Merton, Thomas. *The Seven Storey Mountain.* San Diego: Harcourt Brace, 1948.

Monahan, Sister Molly. *Seeds of Grace: Reflections on the Spirituality of Alcoholics Anonymous.* New York: Riverhead, 2001.

Newton, John. *Amazing Grace.* Olney, England: Olney Hymns, 1779.

Rahner, Karl. "Christianity and Non-Christian Religions." In *Theological Investigations.* Volume V: Later Writings. Translated by Karl-Heinz Kruger, 115–34. New York: Herder and Herder, 1983. [German original 1962].

———. *Foundations of Christian Faith: An Introduction to the Idea of Christianity.* Translated by William V. Dych. New York: Crossroad, 1982 [German original 1976].

Rohr, Richard. *Breathing Under Water: Spirituality and the Twelve Steps.* Cincinnati: Franciscan Media, 2011.

Scorsese, Martin, dir. *Taxi Driver.* Columbia Pictures, 1976.

Second Vatican Council, *Gaudium et Spes* (Pastoral Constitution on the Church in the Modern World). https://www.vatican.va/archive/hist_councils/ii_vatican_council/documents/vat-ii_const_19651207_gaudium-et-spes_en.html

Schleiermacher, Friedrich. *On Religion; Speeches to Its Cultured Despisers.* Translated by John Wood Oman. London: K. Paul, Trench, Trübner, &Co., 1893 [German original 1799].

Shakespeare, William. *Hamlet.* 1603.

Shaw, George Bernard (1924). *Saint Joan: A Chronicle Play in 6 Scenes and an Epilogue.* London: Constable & Co., 1924.

"The Start and Growth of A.A." New York: Alcoholics Anonymous World Services, 2023. https://www.aa.org/the-start-and-growth-of-aa

Tennyson, Alfred Lord. "The Charge of the Light Brigade." In *Maud, and Other Poems.* Boston: Ticknor and Fields, 1855.

Tillich, Paul. *Dynamics of Faith.* New York: Harper and Row, 1957.

Tolstoy, Leo. *What I Believe.* Translated by Constantine Popoff. New York: Cosimo, 2007 [Russian original 1885].

Turteltaub, Jon, dir. *National Treasure.* Walt Disney Pictures, Jerry Bruckheimer Films, 2004.

Tyler, Anne. *Saint Maybe.* New York: Alfred A. Knopf, 1991.

www.ingramcontent.com/pod-product-compliance
Lightning Source LLC
Chambersburg PA
CBHW071722090426
42738CB00009B/1851